To Peter Davey

THE **CITY** **in architecture**

Best wishes from
Rocco Yim
July 03

THE CITY in architecture

First published in Australia in 2002 by
The Images Publishing Group Pty Ltd
ACN 059 734 431
6 Bastow Place, Mulgrave, Victoria 3170, Australia
Telephone (+61 3) 9561 5544 Facsimile (+61 3) 9561 4860
email: books@images.com.au
www.imagespublishinggroup.com

National Library of Australia Cataloguing-in-Publication Data

The city in architecture: recent works of Rocco Design Limited.

Includes index.
ISBN 1 876907 22 3.

1. Rocco Design. 2. Architecture, Modern – China –
Hong Kong. 3. Architecture, Modern I. Title.

720.9512

Edited by Eliza Hope and Kate Ryan
Produced by The Graphic Image Studio Pty Ltd, Mulgrave, Australia
Film by Mission Productions Limited
Printed by Everbest Printing Co., Ltd. in Hong Kong/China

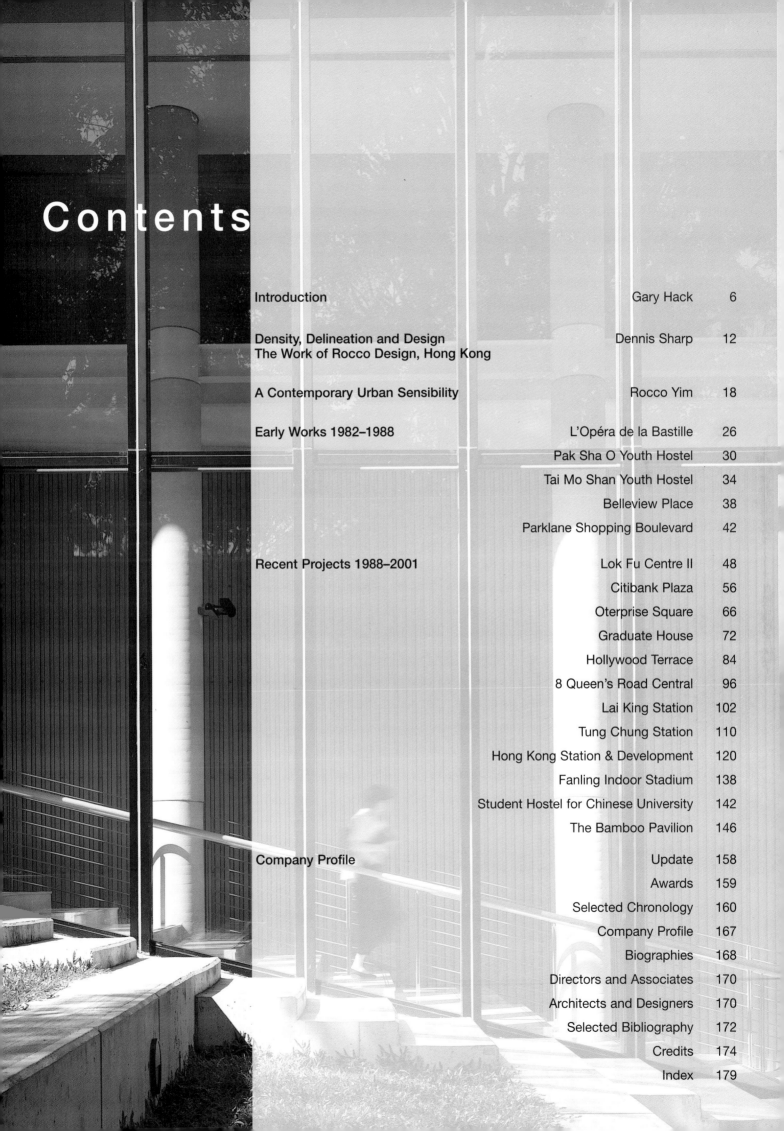

Contents

INTRODUCTION

■■■■■■■ The work of Rocco Design is rooted in a profound understanding of the city where it has been conceived – Hong Kong. Rocco S.K. Yim and his colleagues understand the terrior, as the French say, of the vignerons responsible for their grand crus. Not simply the geography and topography, but also the ways of building, the cultural traditions, the everyday habits and the distinctive ways of seeing and experiencing the city. Like good wine, the buildings of Rocco Design are rooted in all that has gone before, but in ways that are strikingly fresh. And they get better with time.

■■■■■■■ I recall first setting eyes on Citibank Plaza shortly after its completion. How refreshing it seemed in contrast to the ponderous, frontal bank headquarters that had recently opened nearby with great fanfare. Here was a dynamic structure that celebrated the surrounding city, rather than a singular tower standing at attention and ignoring its surroundings. Citibank Plaza deftly mastered the slopes on which it was built, drawing pedestrians through and around its towers. It was designed to be seen close up, with its public spaces revealed to passers-by, but also as an ever-changing structure on the skyline. Its vertical shafts captured the moods of sky and surroundings; at sunset it reflected the golden sunlight, at dusk it glowed and illuminated its environs. It was, to my mind, the first uniquely Hong Kong high-rise. Citibank Plaza was also my first introduction to Rocco Design.

▆▆▆▆▆▆▆▆ Revisiting Citibank Plaza today, a decade after it opened, and surrounded by many additional structures, it still seems to be the perfect response to its site. The special sensibilities evident in this structure have now found their way into many new buildings by Rocco Design in Hong Kong and beyond. This monograph brings them together for the first time, and reveals the attitudes and aspirations of the design partner, Rocco S.K. Yim.

Global Modernism

▆▆▆▆▆▆▆▆ For many years the myth of modern architecture was that its forms could be applied universally, differing only in detail to cope with climate and program. Such buildings spread as global development penetrated each country, and as modernization demanded structures that measured up to those in the most advanced centers of design, places that also happened to be the corporate and financial centers promoting global development. Modernist forms accompanied modern institution: the ubiquitous high-rise office buildings and hotels, new university campuses, performing arts centers or civic structures on public squares. Concrete and steel frames, with glass and metal infill panels, sped the construction process, allowing international companies an almost instantaneous foothold in countries throughout the world. Similar building details could be found in London or Paris or Tokyo or Hong Kong, courtesy of global building material supply networks. The desire to be modern made it possible for New York or Chicago or London architects to work in Hong Kong or Sydney or Manila. But it also made it possible for Hong Kong firms to design buildings in Beijing or Dalian or Vancouver, following their clients as they moved their investments to other shores.

▆▆▆▆▆▆▆▆ The result has been homogeneous islands in virtually every city on the globe – where brand name commercial outlets dominate the ground levels, and managers occupy offices, hotel rooms and apartments above. Each of these new centers is largely indistinguishable from city to city.

Hong Kong Modernism

▆▆▆▆▆▆▆▆ Fortunately, Hong Kong is different. Even with dozens of buildings designed by overseas architects it has managed to maintain an environment that seems unique, that still has the capacity to excite the visitor or resident. For an explanation, we return to demands of the terrior:

small plots of buildable land; soils that require expensive foundations to protect against landslides or subsidence; difficulty in assembling land; and astronomical values for any buildable site. Together they force buildings upward, often in configurations that require complicated plan forms. Views in the dense city command a premium, and buildings are designed to be seen from a distance, particularly from the harbor. The sloping ground plane means that buildings are invariably entered at several levels, and often at great expense, via escalators, bridges or other forms of infrastructure. Tough building regulations in Hong Kong mandate that all apartment rooms have exterior ventilation, resulting in a distinctive and crenellated profile for most residential buildings. This unique collection of rules and norms and necessities has produced a powerful aesthetic that is in the bones of those who live and design buildings in Hong Kong.

The result is a place-centered modernism. Perhaps no building exemplifies this better than Oterprise Square, completed recently by Rocco Design. In the tight confines of the densest part of Kowloon, this sliver office and commercial complex uniquely fits its Hong Kong location. It encourages pedestrians to shortcut the crowded corner, slicing through and revealing a world of offices and shops. At the ground level, the building is as much a passage as a structure – and what a passage! – revealing the building vertically to the pedestrian moving through it. Oterprise Square was one of the first buildings that recognized that the upper, middle and lower portions of a tower each need to respond differently to their context. The top has panoramic views that need to be captured; the middle portion exploits the narrow view angle towards the harbor as defined by adjacent buildings; and the lower levels are the domains of the pedestrian. Buildings of this sort capture the energy of their surroundings, and they are at the heart of how Hong Kong modernism differs from new architecture in most other parts of the world.

Hong Kong is, of course, much more than a city of tall towers climbing up the hillsides as far as roadways and trams will allow. The massive waterfront reclamation areas of the last half-century have produced several new districts on the flats, where many of the old constraints are loosened. Topography and plot size play a role. The waterfront development areas are a world of unlimited possibilities, constrained only by optimism about the economy and the tolerance of developers for risk.

People arrive here by transit, high-speed ferry or train, emerging in sky-lit, air-conditioned concourses. Unfortunately, many of the reclaimed areas have produced 'podium structures' with conventional commercial centers at their base and office or hotel towers above. These are surrounded by elaborate roadways, bridged by endless elevated pedestrian walkways – but with precious few places where pedestrians would choose to stop and linger. And in a climate where high humidity and monsoon rains make outdoors unpleasant much of the year, creating a pleasurable pedestrian world is a special challenge.

■■■■■■■ Rocco Design's plans for the new Hong Kong Station Development in Central rise to the challenge. Generous walkways, plazas and indoor spaces restore civic dignity for the tens of thousands of people who scurry between ferry terminals, trains and mass transit and their workplaces and homes. The completed airport railway station provides an early hint of the quality of places that will be found throughout the development, and the refined detailing of its architecture. Light, from skylights, clerestories and broad expanses of glass, penetrates to the deepest platforms of this many-level city. The surfaces are deliberately monochromatic and machined, allowing the spaces to be animated by the movement of people, trains and taxis, and by the works that inhabit its volume. As with all Rocco Design's buildings, there is a calmness to these spaces that provides a respite from a city that sometimes seems to be on hormones.

Buildings Inspired by Their Situation

■■■■■■■ Fine architecture responds to its context, but is also a creative assemblage of materials in service to a program. Some programs, such as offices, are quite elastic – there can be more or less space, many exterior and interior materials are possible, and many shapes can work equally well. Housing is less forgiving, though. Building rules prescribe the amount of daylight necessary, and life safety requirements dictate distances to exit stairways and many other constraints. The desire for privacy and security constrains ground-level access patterns. Prices are highly competitive, and must account for the costly necessity of garaging automobiles. High land prices in Hong Kong necessitate very high plot ratios, and force designers to stack up many floors of repetitive units. Too often the result is banal – endless estates of housing units stacked from the ground to the sky, with a wasteland at their base.

■■■■■■■■ Hollywood Terrace is a welcome exception. Located on a steeply sloping site, on a well-traveled pedestrian route, it is in reality two distinct archetypes, each a response to its situation. Traversing the 23-meter difference between Hollywood Road and Queen's Road Central is a magnificent set of walkways and plazas, open 24 hours of the day, recreating a new ground level experience of the city. Glass canopies, stair enclosures and elevators bring to life the spaces. The base of the housing estate is so much a part of the city, it is difficult to know where it begins and ends. Above this, sits the second kind of building – refined concrete housing structures that recognize the necessity of repetition, but come to life through their modulation, colors and detailing. They speak to another side of Hong Kong's building legacy – the long-running experiment to invent high-rise housing forms that optimize light, air and views. Rocco Design demonstrates that it can master the discipline of housing, but provide accommodations that are much more than mindless boxes.

■■■■■■■■ Graduate House at the University of Hong Kong illustrates the universality of Rocco Design's response to site and setting. In this case, it is the natural setting of the sloping hillside that gives form and character to the base. Lifting the housing above the treetops allows light and landscape to infuse the public spaces of the conference center and hostel. As in other projects, a grand staircase traverses the slope, making the building a link in the campus network. The housing above has its own discipline, capturing the fine views and providing social spaces on each floor. Simple and unselfconscious detailing emphasizes the richness of experience and detail in this modest-sized building. It is among the finest examples of architecture inspired by its situation.

Beyond Hong Kong

■■■■■■■■ The buildings of Rocco Design illustrated here offer many lessons, and these are not limited to Hong Kong or other rapidly urbanizing Asian cities. They speak of the way in which site and situation can inspire a unique architectural and urban response; how technology and materials, light and procession can be employed to heighten the experience of moving through public places; indeed, how a civic realm can be restored through buildings that take advantage of their special place. They illustrate how buildings can serve multiple purposes, not be thought about as singular responses to their program and site.

Beyond this, calm and mature buildings that aim to uplift everyday experience, rather than become cultural monuments, are a welcome antidote to the extravagant forms and in-your-face architecture that has come to characterize our times. There is much to be learned by careful study of the 17 buildings and projects that follow.

Gary Hack
Dean and Paley Professor
University of Pennsylvania
Philadelphia, Pennsylvania, USA
November 2001

DENSITY, DELINEATION AND DESIGN
THE WORK OF ROCCO DESIGN, HONG KONG

██████████ In his book, The City Assembled, the late Spiro Kostof, whose insights I am particularly moved by, drew attention to the enduring qualities of the urban environment. He wrote: 'Every city has an edge that changes over time ... every city has internal divisions, public places, streets ...'. But, Kostof warned, 'Cities are too particular as phenomena – specific to moments in time and to the vicissitudes of site and culture – to be pinned down by absolute taxonomies'. He could have been speaking of modern Hong Kong rather than the historic examples of cities whose virtues he extols in the subsequent pages of his inspiring book.

██████████ Rocco S.K. Yim, the director of Rocco Design Ltd – who began an architectural practice in 1979 with Rocco Design Associates – displays a full understanding of such broadly based definitions of cities, his views fuelled by many years of practical work in Hong Kong's urban realm. Taxonomies have their place as part of the structure of cities but site, density and culture are unique and specific. Cities are muddied by tradition and by use, and altered by interventions. Classification is for utopians!

██████████ Rocco Yim's work is interventionist. It is forged and sharpened by the experience of working at one of the densest urban coalfaces in one of the world's most rapidly growing contemporary cities. Largely a product of the twentieth century, Hong Kong gives credibility to the term 'the Modern City'. Not only does it look and feel modern, it is extraordinarily prescient in its recent innovative architecture.

Cities in the region of the world in which Rocco Design operates have complicated and complex origins, some of which allude to the Western world, while others do not. But now – within the global village culture in which we live – it is an Asian city, part of a particular tradition but also Western and smothered by that connotation, with all that the term implies. The cities of South-East Asia, based on the technologies forged in the West, are relatively recent assemblies. Hong Kong, it hardly needs saying, is unique. Born of colonialism, it was recently unbound by a new kind of communism.

Rocco Yim adopts a precise attitude to his work; seeing his architecture as 'shaped by the city' rather than the reverse. He claims that architecture itself should decry traditional values in order to be free to reflect contemporary life and values. Thus, he recognizes the way that cities work in the modern world, as precarious, unstable and complex organisms in which – as the world found on 11 September 2001 – chaos and cruelty can become odious partners in the shaping of cities. To take on the city – however familiar it might be to the designer and to use it as a great pictorial canvas – is a modern phenomenon, and of course a very brave act.

Density

Rocco's role as an urban designer, working closely with problems that often exist uniquely in the city, is that of a versatile, dynamic, and above all incisive, conceptual planner. In reflecting on his attitude to work, he has isolated two major issues that have exercised his mind over the years in relation to the unique problems of Hong Kong. The first and quite understandable concern is density. That issue forms the basis for his views about the city as a compact matrix. It leads almost seamlessly into his interest in the organizational structure of modern Hong Kong and its freely flowing transportation systems, its routeways and enviable connective infrastructure.

In an essay of 1985 entitled 'The aesthetics of fluidity', Rocco tells us why these concerns are paramount: 'Hong Kong has a 3-dimensional urban matrix ... roads, paths, decks, bridges and tunnels which knit together the urban fabric – a public realm which works both horizontally and vertically with high fluidity at subterranean levels, at street level, at elevated deck level and reaching up to the topographical mid-levels'.

Usefully he elaborates a functional analysis: 'While the interaction between the public and private realms ... used to be limited to the interface at the building's façade, the advent of modern modes of transport, the adoption of more sophisticated planning mechanisms ... have now resulted, in many instances, in an intentional and 3-dimensional fusion of the two'.

■■■■■■■■ Such views are echoed in the architect's own description of the Lok Fu Centre, a retail complex completed in the early 1990s, which connects directly with the ambiguous conditions of the Wang Tau Hom area. He writes: '... the architecture is an inside-out process, where a contiguous series of connector spaces in various guises; bridge, atrium, open deck, subway are composed as a continuous route that knits together the social, traffic, circulation and open space systems in the neighbourhood'. This leads, he observes, to the public participation of people in the city and in its dynamic, vibrant, open and closed events. Such an anticipatory attitude to the design of public spaces is seen in Rocco's remarkable scheme for the competition for the Opéra de la Bastille in Paris in 1983, in which he was awarded joint First Prize. It was a project of great originality, which opened up a curved external area for the public, echoing the shape of the Colonne de Juillet at the centre of the rondpoint. This was then taken up in plan and section, producing a back-to-back auditorium. One can only add that his later work in Hong Kong has continued to develop since the Opéra. However, the competition entry (an honourable mention) for the Bibliotheca Alexandriana in Egypt was less successful, owing perhaps a little too much to the grouping of architectural elements fashionable in the late 1980s. On this issue, as can be seen in the model of the library, he makes himself clear by claiming a loose association with the Anglo/US postmodernists. However, on the whole he seems to spare little thought for their superficial posturing, their historicizing or the deceptive desire for a world of pastiche. Rather, through his work, Rocco advocates a separate and incremental developmental approach for the concepts he devises.

■■■■■■■■ First, we see that he is basically a pragmatist responding directly to local constraints but also seeking innovation in his designs. This results in economic and practical solutions for large-scale urban problems, whether hotel extensions, shopping boulevards, airport stations or football stadia.

■■■■■■■■ Second, he seeks to develop an idiom or 'image' of one kind or another in keeping with the dynamics and excitement created by 'high' and intense density:

'... success has bred density and it seems density breeds further success', he has claimed.

▬▬▬▬▬ Third, in the links his buildings make with the existing city, one can detect a deeply felt desire for the establishment of real and viable connections and, in much the same sense, with the regional context in which they reside. He expresses something of this desire in the thoughtful 1998 article included in this book, 'A Contemporary Urban Sensibility'.

▬▬▬▬▬ I would like to draw the reader's attention to the section in this article that speaks of Hong Kong and Complexity Theory. Here, Rocco writes of the precariousness and anxiety of Hong Kong. He expresses the fear that it could easily be overwhelmed by its 'explosive concentration and density' caused largely by local topographical conditions as well as its reputation as an 'anarchic' place. It is all the more reassuring to see that these observations have been effectively translated into the reality of Rocco Design's buildings, with projects very much in the modernist vein such as the indoor stadium at Fanling and the truly participatory – public and private – design of the Hong Kong Station Development project, where in essence, density and infrastructure issues coalesce and the public are the main beneficiaries.

Delineation

▬▬▬▬▬ During the early days of the modern movement in architecture the pioneers of a new approach to urban design were concerned with the nature and form of the city. Many of the pioneers felt that the old kind of city – into which it was quite rightly anticipated an enormous influx of new citizens would invade its often-walled perimeter – was the result of a slow natural evolutionary process. It was argued that this process had to be accelerated. The Athens Charter (CIAM 1933) was the key document on functional city design to come out of the early modernist years, the effect of which – despite new and clearly necessary previsions and revisions – still influences architects and urbanists today, determining socio-functionalist approaches to the city. Despite the fact that the Athens Charter was ill-conceived in the first place (it was an antidote to the problems of 35 European cities) the creation of commercial 'functional' zones in cities was one of its platforms. Perhaps pragmatic and analytical but the fact is that such a provision was guided by economic considerations and by architecture. As Reyner Banham remarked, architecture is directly related to land values.

▬▬▬▬▬ One of the key factors in the modernists' (principally Le Corbusier's) argument for a new urbanism was for a streetless urbanity, and one that acknowledged the significance of tall buildings in the open-air and the park. What started with theory was later to be uniquely brought to life in a number of new settlements; ranging from the Italian Modernists at Sabaudia, the British postwar New Towns, Ernst May's Frankfurt and the Corbusian-inspired work of the London County Council Housing Department, to the extraordinarily articulate, functional and structural diagrams of new utopian cities such as Brasilia and Chandigarh. That was fine as far as it went. But this kind of city soon became boring in its predictability. The exercises were completed to a flow of follow-ups from Nigeria to Florida. The new city was delineated but it ignored the relevance of the dense older cities.

Le Corbusier's Plan Voisin and the English MARS Group's attempts to gouge out the existing centres of Paris and London were brave and exciting concepts at the time although clearly ambitiously misguided. They ignored the existing fabric of these cities, which could only be reconditioned and renewed after redundancy, bombing and deterioration had set in. Opportunities to provide areas of development through demolition and by the acquisition of new areas of land led inevitably, it seems, to the issue of density and what the Malaysian architect Ken Yeang calls 'Intensity'. Both Yeang and Rocco have put their fingers on a key factor: the relationship between the closed private worlds and the open public zone of the ubiquitous high building or skyscraper. In Hong Kong the three-dimensional matrix is more advanced than that of many other cities. It has an interconnected infrastructure that links many parts of the urban fabric. Movement in this situation is a key factor for developing design ideas.

Design

There is another side to the story of Rocco Yim. I came across his work after a week's intense discussion and judging in Paris some years ago for the new Opéra de la Bastille. It was only revealed later that one of the many anonymously submitted designs was for a carefully developed and placed urban scheme for the site at the Arsenal by Rocco Yim.

More recently, in a scheme somewhat reminiscent of the Spanish-born architect Santiago Calatrava's Kuwaiti Pavilion at the Seville World Fair, Rocco Yim erected a Bamboo Pavilion for the 'Festival of Vision: Hong Kong' in Berlin in 2000. Using traditional bamboo that provided a symbolic association with China, the temporary building created a memorable impression of unity and harmony. It was a structure where 'the bamboo pavilion is virtually permeable, with the bamboo members being at once structure, enclosure and spatial delineator ...'. There were over 400 pieces of bamboo for this structure, which was situated in the shadow of Hugh Stubbins's much criticized and still pregnant-looking House of Culture. The pavilion was used for drama, music and fashion shows during the festival and for some time afterwards.

██████████ In conclusion, I would like to return to my theme of the non-aligned, non-taxonomic attitude to design, by emphasizing that complexity or chaos is a given condition in Hong Kong. It is an attribute of the city; it underlines its unpredictability and its excitement yet it is its greatest strength. Complexity is its most enduring component, which, in the case of Rocco Design, has not resulted in a bout of monumentalism, nor attracted the design group to any overt symbolism or slavish stylistic reproduction. However, as members of the global community we all have to be truly serious-minded about the world we live in, mindful that the positive side of city life is its compactness and intensity. The city has a sustainable future. Urban design and regeneration can be seen as the keys to an effective translation of sustainable issues into physical realities and used for architecture's own long-term survival. But we will have to take into account not just the national, regional and local issues but the wider obligations brought about by architecture's and our own role in the biosphere. Again, Ken Yeang writes in an important book, The Green Skyscraper, 'we have certain obligatory relationships with the ecosystem and its processes. The built environment and the intensive (i.e. High Density) large urban building should be integrated and have compatible symbiotic relationships with the ecosystems'. Wise words. They form a fitting testimony to an introduction to the work and architectural achievements of Rocco Design which itself seeks to elaborate and articulate such aims.

Dennis Sharp

Dennis Sharp is a British architect, teacher and writer. Formerly senior lecturer at the AA School 1968–82, he was founder editor of AA Quarterly and World Architecture. He is a professor of the International Academy of Architecture, a co-director of CICA (International Committee of Architectural Critics), a Freeman of the Worshipful Company of Chartered Architects, and a former RIBA Vice President. He has lectured widely and presided over architectural awards from Finland to Morocco, served on the juries of the Opéra de la Bastille and in 2001 on the Acropolis Museum Competition in Athens.

February 2002

A CONTEMPORARY URBAN SENSIBILITY

████████████ Once, in an age less given to the universality of values and aspirations than ours, tradition shaped our lives, our lives shaped our architecture, and architecture shaped our cities. This simple linear relationship vanished at some point during the last half century, and since then, **an apparent identity crisis has tormented our collective consciousness.**

████████████ But if tradition is understood as a set of indigenous attitudes, responses and expectations pertaining to specific problems and challenges in a defined space-time, then it is not only obvious, nor perhaps necessarily regrettable, that the role it plays in our lives will diminish. On the threshold of the new millennium, problems and challenges have become global rather than local, such as the looming hegemony of technology, the irreversible depletion of natural resources and the artificial tempering of ecosystems. Feelings become increasingly shared across boundaries, spurred on by an international and instantaneous information network. Most of us actually take pride in being part of the global community, considering ourselves modern cosmopolitan beings first, and Asians, or Chinese, second. Past tradition's influence on our way of living, and therefore our architecture, lies no longer in the physical or ritualistic realm, but rather comes in the guise of a set of spiritual values and sensibilities, which is subtle rather than overt, felt rather than seen.

■■■■■■■■ Not that I dispute the past still lies at the heart of our being. What and who we once were still influence the way we evaluate morals and aesthetics, and the way we react to events and crises. But I believe that, except in a situation where the actual presence of physical heritage contributes to our contemporary built form as a contextual reference, such contribution is otherwise confined to a metaphysical level. I would suggest that the identity of our architecture inevitably owes more to our on-going tradition, embodied most distinctly in our current urban condition. This, I believe, offers that vital regional otherness within globalization that provides the necessary energy to re-invigorate architecture.

■■■■■■■■ **Where once architecture gave shape to the city, it should now be shaped by the city.** The identity of our architecture should be derived not from tradition as frozen fragments of history, but from on-going tradition as evidenced in our contemporary way of living, our current habits and our conscious response to the constraints, challenges and potentials posed by urban habitation; from the way the city works, either by intent or adaptation. Louis Kahn said that one should ask a building what it wants to be. Maybe we need to first ask the city, which now precedes architecture, what it wants its buildings to be.

■■■■■■■■ It is almost conventional wisdom to observe that, as a city, Hong Kong always exists on the edge of chaos, but if there is validity in the complexity theory, it is precisely this unstable and precarious state that generates the energy and stimulus for it to thrive. Perhaps the state of anxiety and precariousness is at the heart of modernity, and certainly in Hong Kong this is invariably associated with politics and finance, but it also manifests in the physical. The city has always been on the verge of being overwhelmed by its explosive concentration and density, and the fact that **the compact matrix is actually mapped onto a tightly confined and three-dimensional terrain,** with a constant strife between permanence and transience, and between the desire for cohesiveness and the pull towards fragmentation. This dissonance and density, paradoxically, has brought forth dynamic energy rather than gridlock, and has resulted in spontaneous vitality of chanced events and happenings rather than stagnation. This has to do, in a large part, not with our heterogeneous built forms, but with the interstices that, existing within and without them, ultimately unify them. **The public realm, functioning in that in-between, demonstrates a high degree of fluidity and elasticity,** whether it be traditional forms such as streets, terraces and alleyways or contemporary spatial types like bridges, decks, galleria, atria, subways, what I call 'urban connectors', and is instrumental in making a city in this dense and apparently anarchic state function.

More so than any other Asian metropolis, Hong Kong learned long ago, perhaps subconsciously at first, that mobility is the key to ultimate freedom and power. The city's urban connectors, some by expedience, others by intent, have now grown from simple disjointed linear elements into a multi-directional and multi-dimensional network. This network strides across the public and private domains, contributing on a fundamental level to the fluidity of movement, but also transcending it to an optimal interaction of the planned and the spontaneous. In this sense, these urban connectors are like arteries, supplying not only nutrition for the city to operate, but also oxygen for its intellect to stay alert. As one of the characteristics of unstable systems, or objects on the edge of chaos, is the indeterminacy of its marginal condition, so the state of indeterminacy and fluidity is an intrinsic character of these connectors in our contemporary urban situation. **They act like chameleons, assuming different guises in response to the demands of the occasion and the varying conditions of density,** changing according to the time of the day or day of the week its role, ambience and perceived shape.

Hong Kong's architecture has, as usual, been slow to respond to the presence of the city and in particular the infiltration of this novel format of the public realm, around which the city now functions. Orthodox modernism has taught us to be primarily concerned with objects in isolation, a classicist approach in attitude if not in form. Postmodernism has been too preoccupied with looking backwards at tangible forms of tradition, arguably asking all the right questions but coming up with all the wrong answers. Deconstruction, on the other hand, in its obsession with a dissolution of architectural endeavour into an outspoken nihilism, is being too conscious of itself.

I have been attempting for some time now to pursue an architecture which connects with the city's presence and demonstrates a contemporary urban sensibility. This is an architecture which deals with relationships rather than the self and which therefore is evolved from contents rather than language or style. **I look for an architecture which invites participation, embracing the new public realm that seeks a blurring of the boundary between architectural objects as traditionally conceived and a virtual fusion between the private and the public.** I am seeking an architecture that is permeable to the city, one that reconciles the theme of convergence and dissipation to its fragmented and dissonant phenomena and in the process promotes interaction under conditions of shifting consciousness.

Seen in this light, the act of making architecture in the contemporary metropolis is both a rational and a personalized event. Rational because the creation of architecture for a specific site is a process of discovery and critique, entailing an objective evaluation of the forces governing the locale and of the site's role in the overall urban picture. Personalized because the ultimate prioritizing of the contextual concerns and, more importantly, the vision of the future interaction between architecture and city remains very much an individual perception.

The architecture of Lok Fu Centre, completed in 1991, is a vision of the building as an anchor in the then fragmented and disjointed area of Wang Tau Hom. The conception of the architecture is an inside-out process, where a contiguous series of connector spaces in various guises, bridge, atrium, open deck, subway are composed as a continuous route that knits together the social, traffic, circulation and open space systems in the neighbourhood. Without an apparent beginning or end, the route becomes the stage for the participation of the city, taking on an obvious receiving and dispersing role, and at times transforming itself into private realms to demonstrate a containing function, holding receptions, bazaars, performances. The indeterminacy, permeability and elasticity of this semi-private/public element, endowed with a temporal quality through its interaction with the light and sky, actually upstage the primary element, that is, retail, for which this building was originally commissioned.

Both Citibank Plaza and Graduate House, completed after Lok Fu, continue this inside-out process of design, where the theme of the indeterminate urban route, and the notions of mobility and connectivity, generate the architecture. One is in the heart of urban Central and the other in a university campus, which is actually a city in microcosm. Because of the composite nature of the programme for these projects, however, there is a simultaneous outside-in process in the shaping of the envelope in response to issues of formal context and environment. The resulting tension, generated by the final resolution of these two opposing processes, is evident in the dynamic dissonance of the architecture and spatial configuration.

███████████ The housing development of Hollywood Terrace in the Hollywood Road urban renewal project plays with an apparent permeability in the architecture rather than actual permeability, taking into account an added concern for spatial defensibleness.

███████████ The Hong Kong Station Development project, on the other hand, takes up more literally the notion of participation and permeability. It expounds them to the fullest extent, since the development is of such a massive scale that meaning can only be derived if it is conceived as a mini-city. This is where the private matrix of offices, hotels, apartments and retail overlap fully and intertwine with the public matrix of podium open space, pedestrian walkway network, station terminal, ground transportation facilities, subway movement system and underground railway system. The proposal for the centrepiece of the development, a 400-metre-high landmark tower, is evolved from an intense engagement with local actualities and the micro/macro shapes of the city, rather than the self-centred structural and technical determinants which usually predominate in the design of such super-towers.

███████████ Another project where the architecture is, in the end, more shaped by the city than the structural and technical agenda, despite the latter's usual predominance in such building types, is the Indoor Stadium at Fanling. Here the structural form is actually manipulated to respond to the perceived movements and relationships in the neighbourhood. There is an inevitable return to the themes of connectivity and permeability, which are instrumental in anchoring this public building in the future civic centre of the once visually anonymous town.

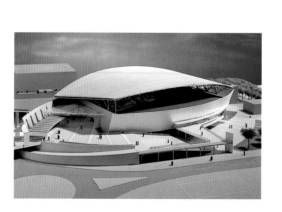

███████████ 1997 was a momentous year (though not for the reason, as it turned out, that we in Hong Kong had self-centredly anticipated). 1997 will be remembered as the year when the Asian economic crises erupted and globalisation of information and money movement firmly established themselves in the world psyche. The term 'globalisation' struck us forcefully with a new meaning and a new reality. The world, henceforth, is, as they say, truly postmodern.

▬▬▬▬▬ Architecturally, I embrace this new postmodernism, an authentic position which takes as its point of departure, not preoccupation with nostalgia but an emphasis on constructive engagement with divergent actualities within globalisation, informed by the presence of the city and tempered by a renewed urban sensibility.

Rocco Yim
December 1998

'Ours is a city where things occur in **close proximity,** and I have come to regard architecture, since our early days, as essentially an **art of relationship**:
between the **old** and the **new**;
between the **natural** and the **man-made**;
between the **physical** and the **ephemeral.**'

Early Works 1982–1988

L'Opéra de la Bastille

Pak Sha O Youth Hostel

Tai Mo Shan Youth Hostel

Belleview Place

Parklane Shopping Boulevard

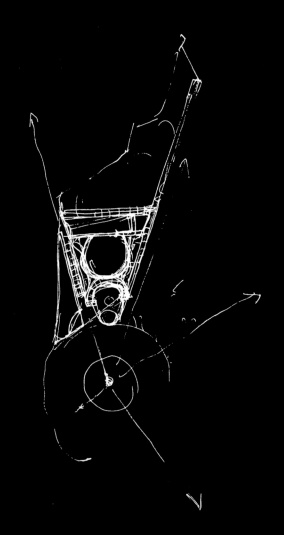

The Opéra de la Bastille is **about three relationships:**
That between the art of opera and the people;
That between Paris's past and present;
and that between architecture and place.

L'OPÉRA DE LA BASTILLE, PARIS
INTERNATIONAL COMPETITION 1983
FIRST PRIZE AWARD

This international competition was organised by the French Cultural Ministry in 1983 to design a new US$250 million 2700-seat opera house at the Place de la Bastille, Paris, in preparation for the celebration of the bicentenary of the 1789 Revolution. It attracted a record 744 entries from 50 countries. A 20-member jury, comprising international artists, critics and architects including Pierre Boulez, Dennis Sharp, Carlo Aymonino, Hermann Hertzberger and Mario Botta shortlisted six entries, from which, eventually, three first prize winners were announced. The entry submitted by Rocco Design Partners was one of the three. Subsequent to the award, another first prize entry by the Canadian architect Carlos Ott was eventually selected for execution, and the new opera was completed in 1990.

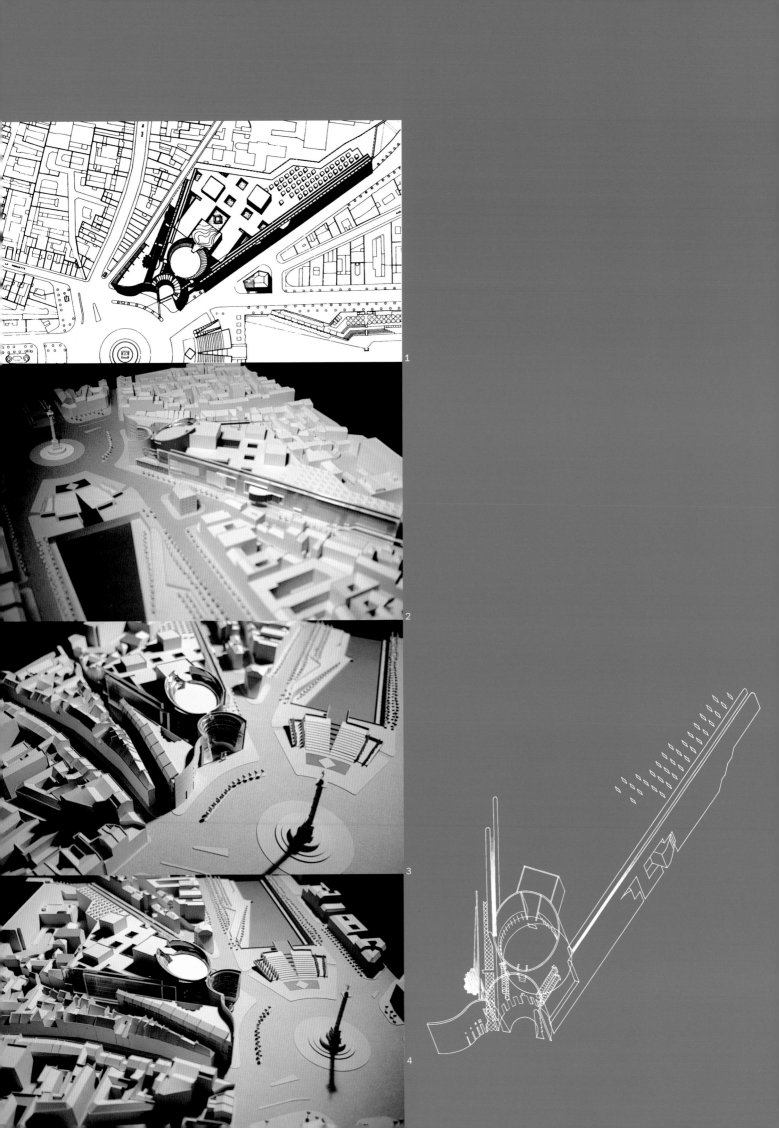

1

2

3

4

1   Context
2,4   Transparent flanks inserted into the city
3,5   Acknowledging the Place

5

The New Opéra de la Bastille

The new Opéra de la Bastille is three things in one. It is a transparent, self-revealing organism for the opera and the performing arts. It is a memorial to the Bastille in particular and the French Revolution in general. It is also a significant urban infill.

The Opera as an Urban Infill

The design of the opera addresses both the general and the specific urban contexts. It makes, as it must do, a strong formal gesture towards the Place and the Colonne de Juillet. It respects the neighbouring streets and buildings, their typology, scale and texture. It reaffirms the existing streets' axes, maintaining their linear edge and that sense of urban boundary characteristic of traditional cities. It aims, above all, to contribute towards the process of revitalisation of the district, creating along and reinforcing the axis generated by the Colonne, a new street that penetrates the opera. Completely pedestrianised, this new street generates activities, sustains them 24 hours a day and allows the famous 'human qualities' of the Parisian streets to permeate the environment, encouraging greater participation of the public in the events of the opera. In much the same way Montmartre was for young artists at the turn of the century, so this new street will be a venue for young musicians, for the rest of this century and the next, to meet, communicate, aspire to and explore.

The Opera as a Memorial

Located on a site of historical as well as urban significance, and in its attempts to enhance the status of the district as the cradle of the French Revolution, the opera, by necessity, serves as a memorial. Its architecture accommodates and integrates with historical references, abstract, symbolic or metaphoric. The principal entrance façade facing the Place de la Bastille forms a complementary backdrop to the Colonne de Juillet, the symbolic V-configuration

that rises from its base celebrates the enduring nature and the ultimate triumph of what it represents. The heavy curved wall adjacent to the entrance façade suggests the old Bastille prison wall, being constructed from the same stone (if possible) as the old prison, and with the same cell-like windows. Its crudely broken edge (metaphoric of its destruction) gives way to the street, a street speaking of history and progress. Historically significant figures and objects of the 1789, 1830 and 1848 Revolutions are lined along the street, together with figures of famous musicians and composers, placed according to a common time scale.

The Opera as a Transparent Organism

The opera is, above all, a liberated and democratised place of performance. In contrast to tradition, be it classical or orthodox modern, where functions are hidden behind ornate façades or monumental blank walls, this new opera opens itself up, becomes extroverted and invites comprehension. The entrance forecourt, which is surrounded on three sides by transparent slanting glass walls, is essentially a preparatory space, preparing one's mood for the occasion. Spatially and figuratively, it is the auditorium turned inside-out, making a welcoming gesture to the audience and embracing it. Thus, those who approach find themselves, apparently, on centre stage before even starting to enter. All circulation areas, foyers, passages and corridors, public and private, where exchanges and contacts tend to take place most in an opera house, are fully transparent to the people in the street. The moods of the audience and the performers, before and after performances, are radiated outwards, through the transparent skin, to the surrounding neighbourhood. In the new pedestrian street people gather, sit, drink, contemplate backstage activities, watch simultaneous transmission of performances on giant screens, applaud and respond. An evening of excitement at the opera is thus not confined to those with tickets inside the auditorium, nor only for the duration of the show. It overflows onto the streets and lingers on into the night, beckoning for active and passive involvement by passers-by, creating an increased interaction with the masses not only on but also off stage.

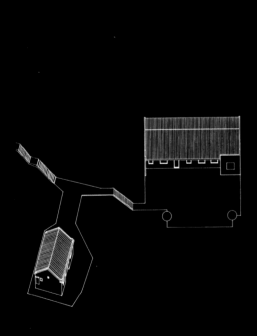

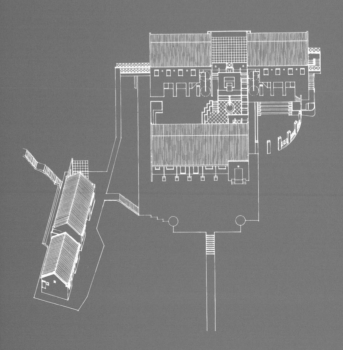

Relating **rural** vernacular to **contemporary** architecture;
relating **aged** shell to **new** neighbours and new use.

PAK SHA O YOUTH HOSTEL
SAI KUNG, HONG KONG
DESIGNED 1982, COMPLETED 1985
HKIA PRESIDENT'S PRIZE 1986

Pak Sha O Youth Hostel is situated in one of the last areas of Hong Kong to retain a rural character. The extension involved the conversion of the original single-storey building into the big common/dining building and the addition of two double-storey dormitory blocks and a new warden's quarters.

The essence of the design is the attempt to capture the traditional rural village flavour and integrate it with a modern architectural language. The traditional concepts of courtyards, semi-enclosed spaces and the sequence of spaces are introduced by manipulating the relationship between the new and the existing building blocks and the relationship between the new envelope and the existing structure. The introduction of elements like the lily pond, planters, trellis and pergolas serves to bring nature more closely into contact with the built forms, and in so doing fosters a more receptive mood for their appreciation.

Client: Hong Kong Youth Hostels Association
Structural Engineer: Peter K.C. Pun & Associates
Geotechnical Engineer: Siu Yin Wai & Associates
Main Contractor: Chuen Lee & Co.
Construction Cost: HK$2.3 million

1

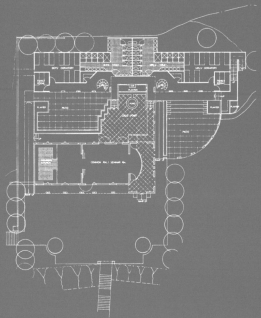

2

1   View of inner courtyard
2   Ground level plan
3   Relationship between existing (foreground) and the added (backdrop)
4   View of courtyard from communal block
5   Entrance to communal block
6   Communal block lobby

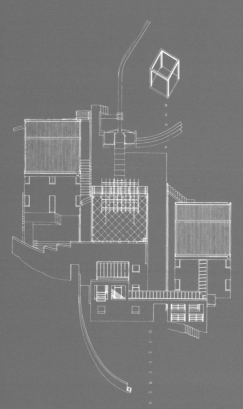

Establishing physical and spatial **linkage** between existing building and new addition; exploring the **relationship** between the man-made and the natural.

TAI MO SHAN YOUTH HOSTEL
TSUEN WAN, HONG KONG
DESIGNED 1985, COMPLETED 1988

The site for this hostel is a plateau near the crest of Tai Mo Shan, Hong Kong's tallest mountain. With a panoramic view towards predominantly virgin landscape, and subject to more frequent changes in mood of weather (mist, rain, sunshine) than most parts of the territory, the site has a tranquil, almost surreal ambience.

The original hostel consisted of a single purpose-built girls' dormitory only, while the boys' dormitory is located in an out-of-use barrack and the communal block in a temporary shed. The extension involves the addition of a new boys' dormitory and a new communal block, and they are carefully sited so that all the blocks are interlinked by level covered passages, protected from the sometimes unusually damp weather and accessible to disabled people. The resulting open spaces, defined between the old and new blocks, are carefully landscaped to create hierarchies and different identities, which combine to contribute towards a sense of place.

Client: Hong Kong Youth Hostels Association
Structural Engineer: BMP Civil & Structural Engineers Ltd.
Main Contractor: Chuen Lee & Co.
Construction Cost: HK$2.4 million

1,2 Landscape details
3   Linkage between blocks
4   Communal block detail
5   Main level plan
6   View of communal block
7   Main approach to hostel;
    communal block to the left;
    existing dormitory to the
    right

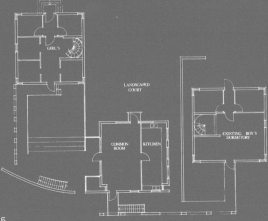

GIRL'S

LANDSCAPED
COURT

COMMON
ROOM

KITCHEN

EXISTING BOY'S
DORMITORY

5

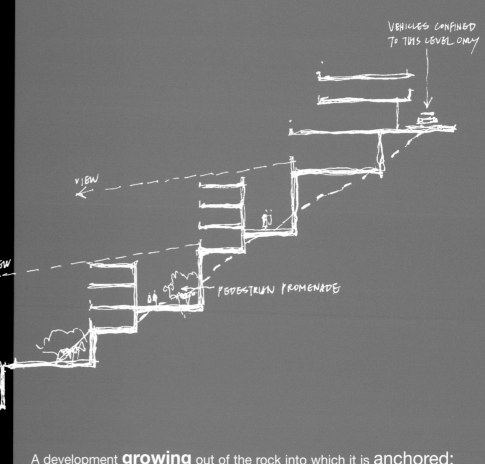

VEHICLES CONFINED
TO THIS LEVEL ONLY

VIEW

VIEW

PEDESTRIAN PROMENADE

POOL

A development **growing** out of the rock into which it is **anchored;**
the form, massing and siting all directly **related** to the **quest** for
that invaluable distant view of Repulse Bay.

BELLEVIEW PLACE

BELLEVIEW DRIVE, REPULSE BAY, HONG KONG

DESIGNED 1985, COMPLETED 1988

This is a residential development for 15 houses and 14 duplex apartment units. Located on the slopes above Repulse Bay, the site is characterised by steepness remarkable even in Hong Kong and by the obstruction of extensive existing developments in front. The site planning therefore relies on a 45-degree rotation of the axes of the main functional areas of each house, on a stepped platform arrangement down the slope, in order to gain views for the majority of the units towards the sea or the distant green hills. Vehicular access is restricted to the uppermost platform, while a centrally located lift provides level pedestrian access to all the units at the lower levels.

The concept of the massing takes its hint from the typology of the Mediterranean hill town, with the architecture apparently growing out of the rock on which it is founded. Each unit has a high degree of individuality and autonomy, yet each is bound to the others by an overall sense of community.

Client: The Great Eagle Project Management Ltd
Structural Engineer: Harris & Sutherland (F.E.) Ltd
Quantity Surveyor: WT Partnership
Landscape Consultant: Team 73 HK
Main Contractor: Shui Ho Construction Co., Ltd
Construction Cost: HK$30 million

1   View of development
2,3   Swimming pool details
4   Individual houses with rotated façade
5,6   View of development from base of hill

5

6

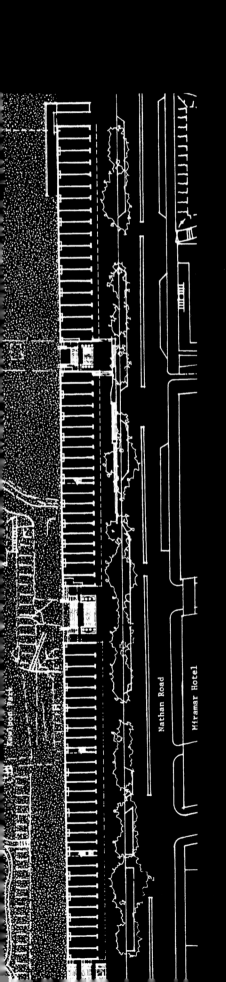

Nathan Road

Miramar Hotel

Defining the **edge** of Kowloon Park and **celebrating** its **connection** with the city, searching for an **appropriate relationship** between the architectural form and the landmark stretch of banyan trees.

PARKLANE SHOPPING BOULEVARD

NATHAN ROAD, TSIMSHATSUI, HONG KONG

DESIGNED 1983, COMPLETED 1985

Parklane Shopping Boulevard is situated on the eastern boundary of Kowloon Park and stretches from one end to the other for more than 370 metres, perhaps horizontally the longest building ever constructed in Hong Kong. It is interrupted at two points along the length by entrances into the renovated Kowloon Park.

Despite the simple programme the new building embodies an urban as well as a social concern. It revitalizes a previously sterile urban environment and provides a new link with the neighbourhoods to the south and north. The shopfronts pose a strong urban presence, flanking a new pedestrian promenade where people are encouraged to stroll, to linger and to enjoy at leisure the magnificent trees and their shade.

Befitting the true status of Kowloon Park in this part of the city, the entrances to the park are dramatised. The entrance portals lure, beckon and welcome, so that entering the park becomes an event.

Client: Lucky City Co., Ltd.
Structural Engineer: P.L. Wong & Associates
Geotechnical Engineer: Paul Tong & Associates
E/M Engineer: Consolidated Consulting Engineers
Acoustics Consultant: Campbell & Shillinglaw
Main Contractor: Tai Yieh Construction Co.
Construction Cost: HK$70 million

1

2

3

1 View of boulevard, park entrance in foreground
2 Linearity of shopfront versus banyan trees
3 Park entrance detail
4 Park entrance, night view

'Since the 1990s, when we started to deal with projects in our urban areas, the term "relationship" has, for us, taken on a wholly **new dimension.**

Preoccupied with the **making of architecture in the city,** I have come to cherish the notion of the **city in architecture.**'

Recent Projects 1988–2001

Lok Fu Shopping Centre II

Citibank Plaza

Oterprise Square

Graduate House

Hollywood Terrace

8 Queen's Road Central

Lai King Station

Tung Chung Station

Hong Kong Station + Development

Fanling Indoor Stadium

Student Hostel for Chinese University

The Bamboo Pavilion

As anchor building in an otherwise fragmented urban area. The architecture incorporating a **seamless** urban route, a **contiguous** series of **connector** spaces that invites the participation of the city.

LOK FU SHOPPING CENTRE II

LOK FU, KOWLOON, HONG KONG

DESIGNED 1988, COMPLETED 1991
HKIA CERTIFICATE OF MERIT 1991
ARCASIA GOLD MEDAL 1994

The site for Lok Fu Shopping Centre II is part of a large parcel of land owned by the Hong Kong Housing Authority in East Kowloon. In the last two decades, development of low-cost high-density housing estates took place to the north of the site, together with a shopping spine that stretched through the estates from north to south, terminating at Wang Tau Hom East Road, where a mass transit railway station was constructed at more or less the same time.

When design commenced on Centre II, the site was virtually isolated from the existing estates and the station by Wang Tau Hom East Road, and there were vague plans only to provide a district open space to the south. From the outset, the design intent was not only to provide the functional accommodation requested by the client, but to make use of the opportunity to stitch together the urban fabric, to reach out and link the various elements in the neighbourhoods together functionally and urbanistically.

Located in an area where a large population is living in public low-cost housing, the new shopping centre is intended to provide a much-needed connection from the housing estates to the various transport modes and to the open recreational areas in the neighbourhood. It is also designed to bring the population daily through a succession of uplifting architectural spaces in the centre, and provide a venue for major shows/events during weekends and holidays. The centre is meant to integrate with the neighbourhoods not only architecturally but spiritually – reflecting and catering for the dynamic energies of a youthful and upwardly mobile population.

Centre II is conceived as an extension, both physically and programmatically, to the existing shopping spine, providing more than 10,000 square metres of retail, cinema and restaurant areas, together with a public carpark and a public transport interchange beneath the pedestrian plaza.

Centre II acts as a keystone building in the neighbourhood, expanding and completing the area's existing open space, circulation and traffic systems. Positioned at the periphery of the existing housing estates, Centre II defines their edge and assumes a transitional role between the estates and the new district park to the south. With an integrated transport interchange and a direct connection to Lok Fu Station, it is, at the same time, a pivotal node for pedestrian traffic, resolving the circulation horizontally and vertically within a skylit atrium space. The atrium also serves as a distribution space for shopping traffic, and this dual role helps to elevate, for the everyday commuter, the mundane exercise of commuter traffic into an uplifting urban experience.

Formally, the architecture of Centre II makes reference to the immediate context. From within the new park, it is an architectural object sitting in an open landscape; its object quality achieved by a deliberate composition of forms. From Lok Fu Estate, it denotes a definite visual conclusion to a sprawling complex, continuing and then arresting the motion set up by its curvilinear circulation spine. Compositionally, the geometrical collage expresses the notion of urban continuity and connectivity, and from the pedestrian plaza its dynamism serves as a backdrop for a variety of human activities.

Client: The Hong Kong Housing Authority
Structural Engineer: Harris & Sutherland (F.E.) Ltd.
E/M Engineer: Associated Consulting Engineers
Quantity Surveyor: Levett & Bailey
Traffic Consultant: MVA Asia
Main Contractor: Shui On Building Contractors Ltd.
Construction Cost: HK$200 million

1

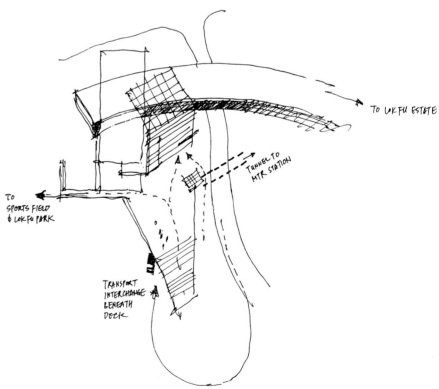

TO LOK FU ESTATE

TUNNEL TO
MTR STATION

TO
SPORTS FIELD
& LOK FU PARK

TRANSPORT
INTERCHANGE
BENEATH
DECK

1 Exterior view;
   pedestrian
   bridge
   penetrating
   the atrium
   from the right
   across Wang
   Tau Hom Road
2 Atrium;
   pedestrian
   bridge entering
   the atrium
   from upper
   right
3 Exterior detail
4 Atrium detail
5 Atrium;
   extension to
   open deck to
   the left

6

7

8

9

6 Exterior view;
bridge link to
public park on
the left

7 Exterior view;
pedestrian
deck spanning
across Wang
Tau Hom Road

8,10
  Atrium with
optimum
natural lighting

9,11
  Pedestrian
movement
through atrium

10

11

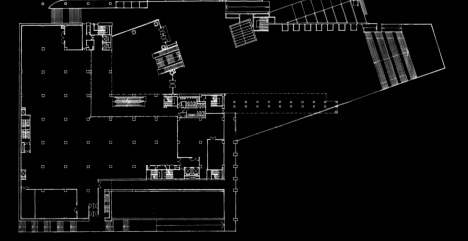

12

13

14

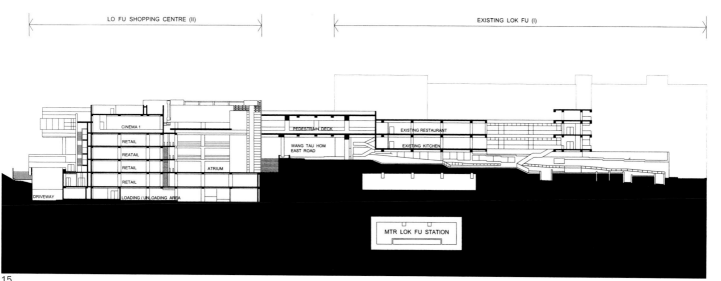

LO FU SHOPPING CENTRE (II)   EXISTING LOK FU (I)

CINEMA 1

RETAIL

REATAIL

RETAIL

RETAIL

DRIVEWAY

LOADING / UNLOADING AREA

ATRIUM

PEDESTRAIN DECK

WANG TAU HOM
EAST ROAD

EXISTING RESTAURANT

EXISTING KITCHEN

MTR LOK FU STATION

15

An urban landmark that **fuses** the public realm with the private via a **fluid** pedestrian network at its base, instilling the architecture with the **presence** of the city.

CITIBANK PLAZA

GARDEN ROAD, HONG KONG
DESIGNED 1989, COMPLETED 1992
HKIA SILVER MEDAL 1994

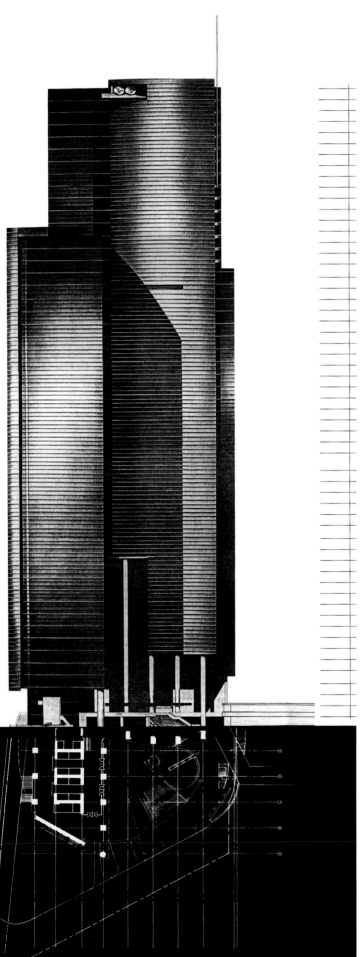

Known better by its lot number 8888, the site for Citibank Plaza is the last major piece of virgin urban land in Central and presents significant design challenges as well as opportunities. On the one hand, it bestrides both the old (i.e. Queen's Road Central) and the new (i.e. Admiralty and Queensway) commercial cores, as well as the immediate mid-levels and the waterfront, offering opportunities for linkage and continuity. On the other, it stands adjacent to Hong Kong's newest and most aggressive landmark, the Bank of China Tower, and calls for an appropriate response.

The solution is a twin-tower development with an asymmetrical configuration, rising to 50 and 40 storeys and forming an L-shape that embraces an open plaza in front. The plaza is in two interlinked levels relating to the topography of the site, and with walkways and footbridges discharging into it from various strategic destination points (i.e. Peak Tram Station, Hong Kong Park, Hilton Hotel carpark, etc.), it actually functions as a pedestrian traffic node for the neighbourhood. While the towers are aligned with the urban axes of the old Central (i.e. St John's Cathedral and Hilton Hotel), the plaza is rotated to respond to the axes of Queensway and the Bank of China Tower, emphasising the visual continuity of the open space all the way down to Chater Garden.

The asymmetrical massing of the twin towers is a tacit acknowledgment and respect for the step-back profile of the Bank of China Tower, and the selected external finishes of silver/grey mirrored glass, natural aluminium cladding and flamed granite base ensure a visual compatibility in surface texture and colour. But the expression of the new towers complements their neighbour through deliberate contrast rather than comformity, and in so doing projects their own identity and character. Instead of sharpness and angularity, it portrays curves and rounded corners; instead of a rigid geometric discipline, it emphasises spontaneous expressions. Aesthetically, it reads as a 'constructive synthesis', a collage and juxtaposition of parts which are apparently unstable and incomplete by themselves, but which interact to compose a dynamic whole – a visual metaphor for the spontaneity and energy of the city's spirit.

Client: Shine Hill (Great Eagle) Development Ltd.
Structural Engineer: Ove Arup & Partners
E/M Engineer: J Roger Preston & Partners
Geotechnical Engineer: Ove Arup & Partners
Quantity Surveyor: Levett & Bailey
Acoustics Consultant: Campbell & Shillinglaw
Lighting Consultant: Tino Kwan Lighting Consultants
Traffic Consultant: MVA Asia
Landscape Consultant: Urbis Travers Morgan Ltd.
Curtain Wall Consultant: Dax Curtain Wall Consultants (HK) Ltd.
Main Contractor: Sung Foo Kee Ltd.
Construction Cost: HK$1,800 million

1 Façade detail
2 Exterior view: Bank of China Tower in the foreground and footbridge to Central to the right
3 Exterior view from the south: HK Park in the foreground
4 Interior atrium between the twin towers
5 Night view

1

2

3

4

6   Escalators in atrium leading to HK Park:
    a 24-hour public passage
7   Link-bridge between twin towers
8   View of atrium from link-bridge: visual
    interface between public and private realms
9   Grand steps to entrance with fully glazed
    atrium beyond

10　View up at atrium soffit

11　View of atrium from link-bridge

12　Link-bridge with view out towards city

13　Interior stair detail

14　Lift lobby

10

11

12

13

14

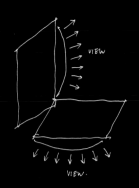

VIEW

VIEW.

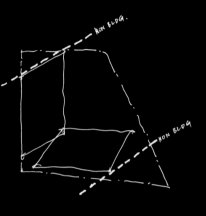

AON BLDG.

AON BLDG

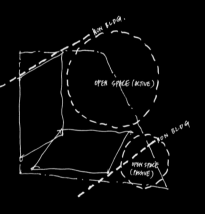

AON BLDG.

OPEN SPACE (ACTIVE)

AON BLDG

OPEN SPACE (PASSIVE)

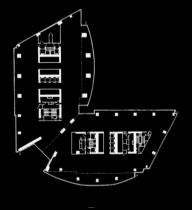

15

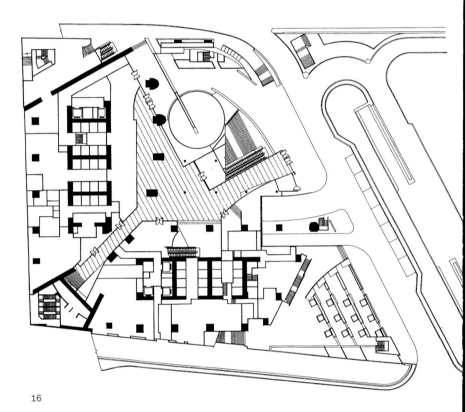

16

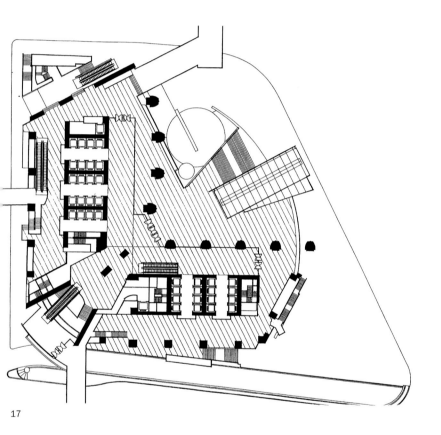

17

18

15 Conceptual sketches
16 Lower ground level
17 Upper ground level
18 Interior detail

A 'contextual' tower where the architecture is **shaped** by the city.

OTERPRISE SQUARE

NATHAN ROAD, KOWLOON, HONG KONG
DESIGNED 1993, COMPLETED 1997

The site is located at the junction of Nathan Road and Middle Road in Tsimshatsui, a traditionally busy commercial and tourist neighbourhood. The site is sandwiched between a number of landmark buildings in the district: the Peninsula Hotel, the Sheraton Hotel and the Hyatt Regency Hotel. It is relatively small in area, only about 1,000 square metres, and what used to be a panoramic view of Victoria Harbour is now largely obstructed by the Sheraton and the newly extended Peninsula Tower.

The redevelopment is envisaged to be a Grade A office building with a retail podium. The challenge to the design is how to exploit fully, under the restrictions of its towering neighbours and its own relatively small area, the potential of the site in this particular 'golden' location.

The strategy in the design of the podium is to introduce a passage cutting diagonally across the site linking Nathan Road and Middle Road, so that pedestrians are tempted to use this shortcut through the retail areas, and be brought, involuntarily, through the skylit atrium above this passage, into visual contact with the various retail levels and the associated bridgelinks and escalators – an intentional mixing and blurring of the boundary between the private and the public domains, resulting in an architecture which is both fluid and permeable.

In the design of the office tower, a conscious attempt is made to maximize the view of the harbour available at the different levels of the tower. This results in the façade being oriented towards the southwest from the sixth to the 13th floor, through the gap between the Sheraton and the Peninsula, and towards the south from the 15th to the 27th floor, once it is clear of the roof of the Sheraton, to capture the whole panorama of Hong Kong Island.

The form of the building is thus predetermined by the above strategies and represents a distinct example of a 'contextual highrise' in the dense urban fabric typical of Hong Kong.

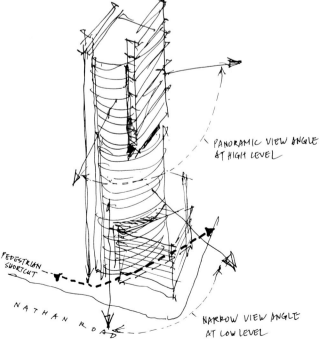

Client: Stelux Holdings International Ltd.
Structural Engineer: Maunsell Consultants Asia
Geotechnical Engineer: Maunsell Consultants Asia
E/M Engineer: Meinhardt (M&E) Ltd.
Quantity Surveyor: Levett & Bailey
Lighting Consultant: Isometrix
Main Contractor: Penta Ocean Construction Co. Ltd.
Construction Cost: HK$271 million

1 Urban shortcut through retail podium
2 Skylight above podium passage
3 Shading detail for south façade
4 Entrance to skylit podium passage
5 The tower in context

6

7

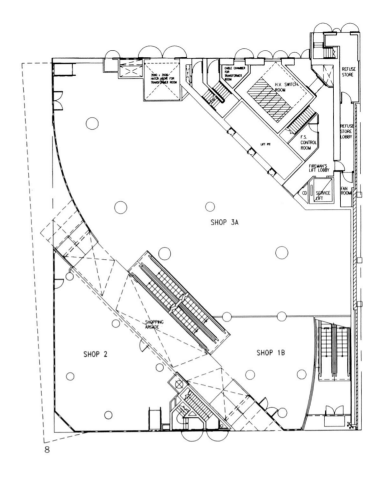

8

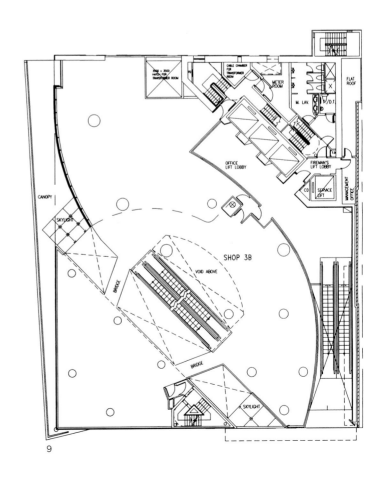

9

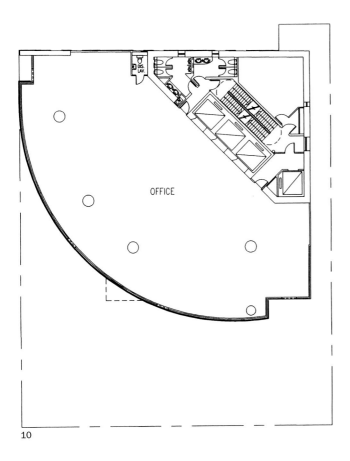

OFFICE

10

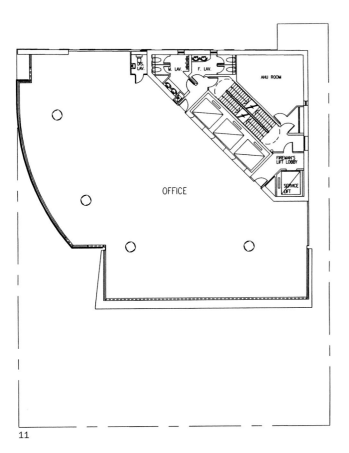

OFFICE

11

6   Podium link-bridge detail
7   Glazed façade detail
8   Ground level
9   First floor (office entrance) level
10 Lower level office plan
11 Upper level office plan

A building that completes the missing link in the sloping campus: the cascading series of permeable and fluid public spaces at its base unite the architecture and the setting.

GRADUATE HOUSE
THE UNIVERSITY OF HONG KONG

POKFULAM, HONG KONG
DESIGNED 1994, COMPLETED 1998
HKIA SILVER MEDAL 1998

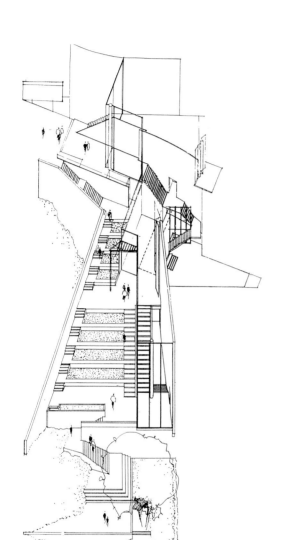

Graduate House is a mixed-use academic building that serves three distinct functions: a dormitory for 210 graduates, an amenity centre for the whole student body and a conference centre for the public.

The design's main aim is to merge the campus into the architecture and to create a green environment both within and without the building envelope. More specifically, the following strategies are adopted:

1. The hostel block is oriented to face south and northeast, with narrow, solid façades and circulation elements as buffers to face east and west, thus achieving appropriate solar insulation and respecting the existing campus planning axes.

2. The footprint of the hostel block is carefully configured to facilitate single-loaded corridors for possible cross-ventilation across all bedrooms, as well as maximal view and natural lighting for the double-volume communal lounges.

3. The existing natural features on site such as the nullah, the valley and the trees are preserved and a more formal landscaped route is created to flank the natural terrain as a green 'connector space' for daily commuters, taking them from the campus centre to the other campus buildings up the slope.

4. A contiguous series of semi-private/semi-public spaces are created at the building's base to unite the architecture; a series of flowing, meandering spaces cascading down from the uppermost level of the slope to the lowest levels. Endowed with a temporal quality through their interaction with natural light and greenery, the visually permeable and fluid nature of the spaces help promote social exchange and contribute to the spontaneity and liberal ambience of campus activities.

Client: The University of Hong Kong
Structural Engineer: Mitchell, McFarlane, Brentnall & Partners Int'l Ltd.
E/M Engineer: Mitchell, McFarlane, Brentnall & Partners Int'l Ltd.
Quantity Surveyor: Levett & Bailey
Main Contractor: Nishimatsu Construction Co. Ltd.
Construction Cost: HK$130 million

1

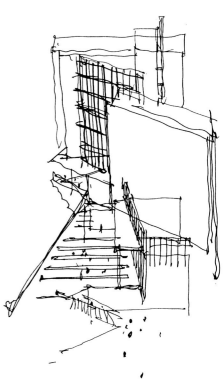

1 External view from base of slope: cascading external terraces flanking glazed
2 Entrance to hostel at upper level
3 View looking down external terraces
4 Glazed interior route
5 Interior route overlooked by hostel lobby

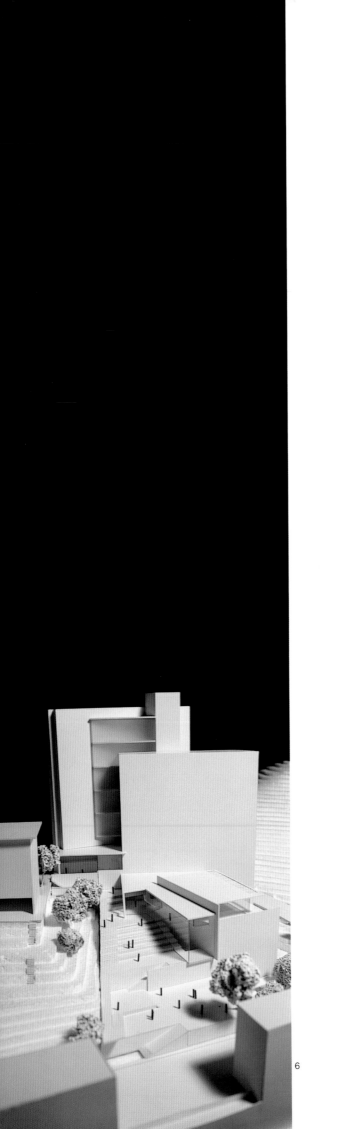

6

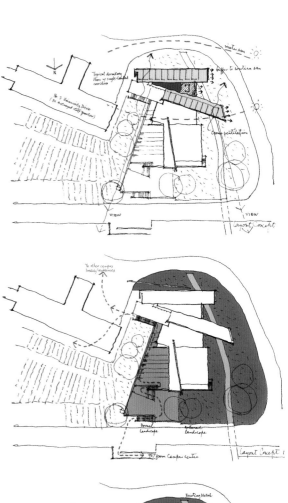

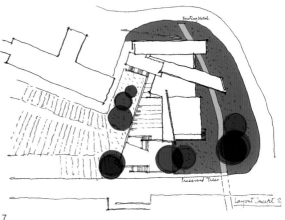

7

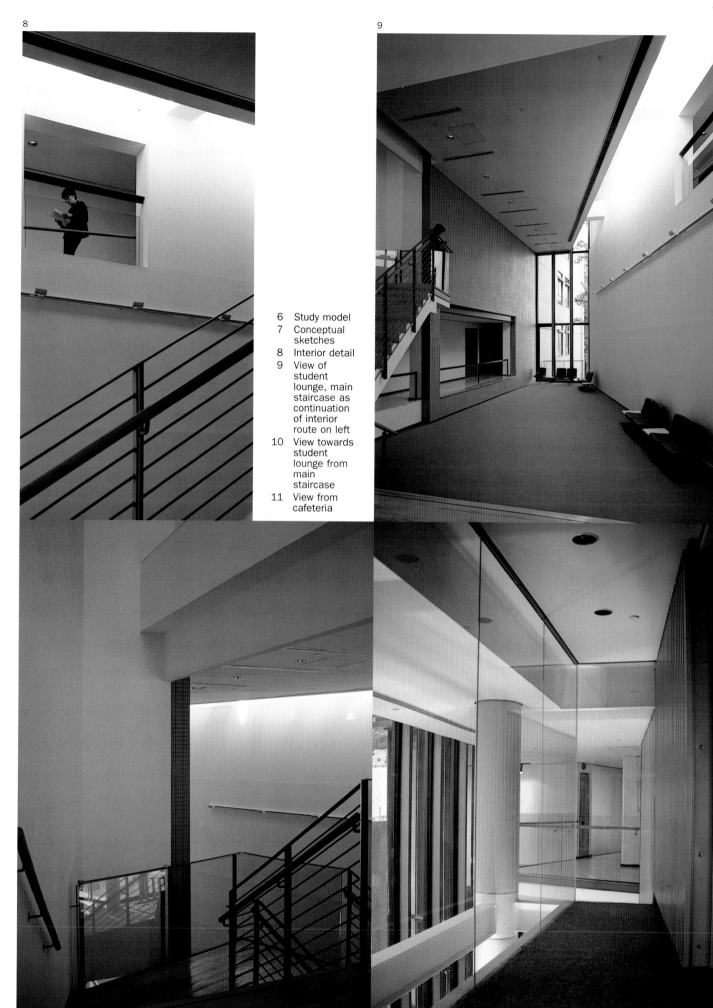

8

9

6 Study model
7 Conceptual sketches
8 Interior detail
9 View of student lounge, main staircase as continuation of interior route on left
10 View towards student lounge from main staircase
11 View from cafeteria

10

11

12 View of interior route
    from external terraces
13 View of external terraces
    from interior route

14

15

16

17

14–18
Play of shadow
and light
enhancing the
quality of
spatial fluidity

19

19 Model
20 Longitudinal section
21 Typical hostel level
22 Main conference centre level

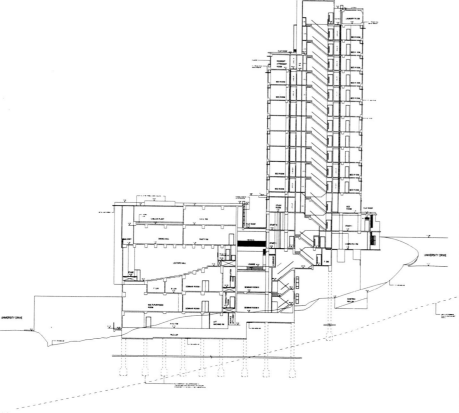

20

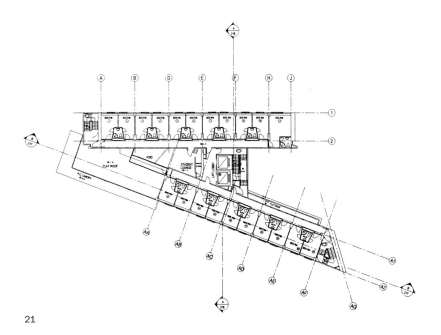

21

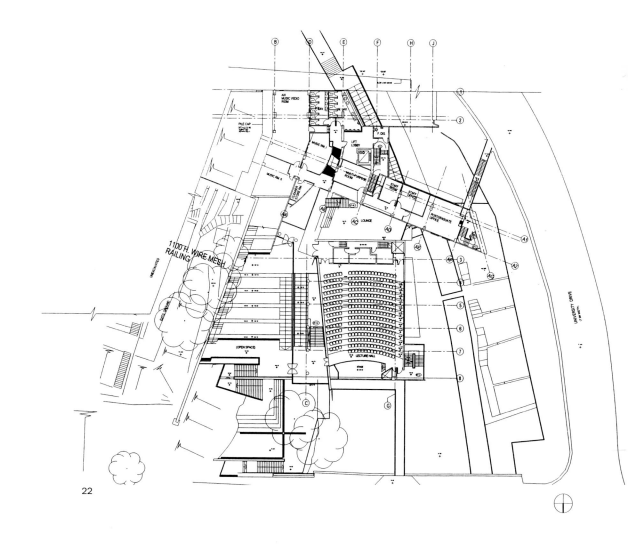

22

A **high-density infill** development against a steep slope in an old part of the urban area, where a **public** route **interwines** with the **private** route up the hill with varying vistas of the city.

HOLLYWOOD TERRACE, URBAN RENEWAL

HOLLYWOOD ROAD, HONG KONG
DESIGNED 1987, COMPLETED 1999
HKIA CERTIFICATE OF MERIT 2001

Situated within the colourful, dense and highly textured urban fabric of old Central/Western districts, and sandwiched between Hollywood Road and Queen's Road Central against a slope with a level difference of 23 metres, the site calls for a careful response in terms of its environment, connection to context and an appropriate interaction between the private and the public realms. On the one hand, it poses a challenge for the development of typically dense residential accommodation with a plot ratio of 9 under highly constrictive environmental and geological constraints. On the other, it offers an opportunity for urban regeneration and integration to complement and complete the existing open space, traffic and circulation systems in the neighbourhood.

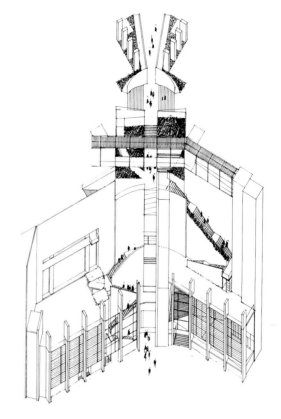

Under the land lease conditions, a certain amount of public space needs to be provided, with part of the lot zoned as a public amenity. These spaces are developed as a landscaped garden and a series of landscaped terraces that, together with stairs and lifts, form part of an elaborate public route connecting Queen's Road Central with Hollywood Road that allows 24-hour pedestrian access through the site. This is carefully interwoven with the private access route for residents, from both Queen's Road and Hollywood Road, to the residential tower lobbies and their own private amenity areas. The two routes intertwine but remain segregated.

The residential section is developed into two towers of 35 storeys. These are, by necessity, typically compact units with eight flats clustered around each core. But the units are carefully configured so that they face predominantly north or south. Overlooking between units is largely avoided and most living areas, despite the small unit size, are capable of being cross-ventilated.

The towers are set back as much as possible from the noisy Queen's Road, which helps to maximise the openness of the podium terraces in front and to alleviate the harshness of the encroaching adjacent buildings. Nevertheless, the visual continuity of the street frontage is maintained, the rhythmical arrangement of vertical piers both along Queen's Road and Hollywood Road makes a subtle reference to the traditional tenement buildings which once proliferated in the neighbourhood. In particular, the row of shop units along Hollywood Road, defined by the piers, are intended to re-connect the line of popular antique shops on either side of the site and to re-affirm Hollywood Road's status as 'the antique street' of Hong Kong.

Client: Hong Kong Housing Society
Structural Engineer: Ove Arup & Partners
Geotechnical Engineer: Ove Arup & Partners
E/M Engineer: Parsons Brinckerhoff (Asia) Ltd
Quantity Surveyor: C.S. Toh & Sons & Associates
Main Contractor: Gammon Construction Ltd
Construction Cost: HK$573 million

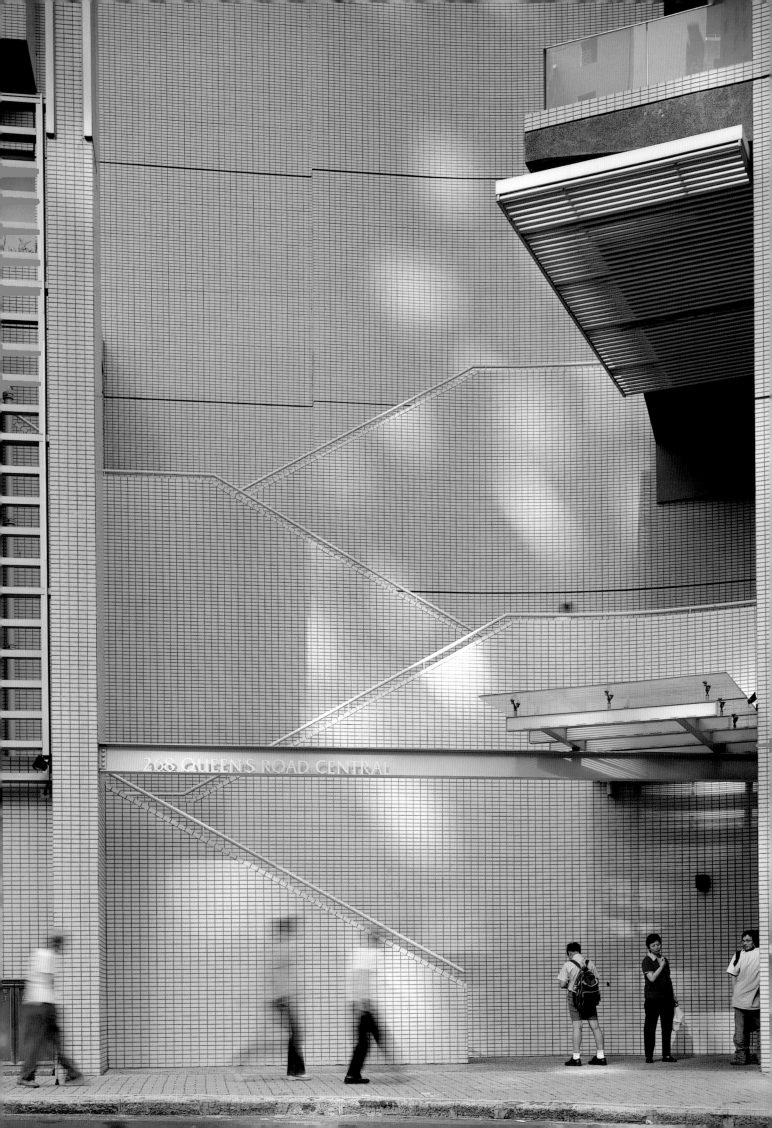

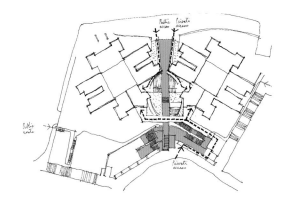

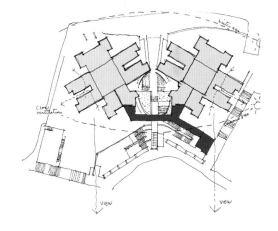

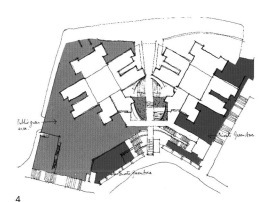

1 The starting point of
  the public route at
  Queen's Road
2 Exterior view of the
  two residential
  towers
3 Night view, private
  residential lobby in
  the foreground
4 Conceptual diagrams

4

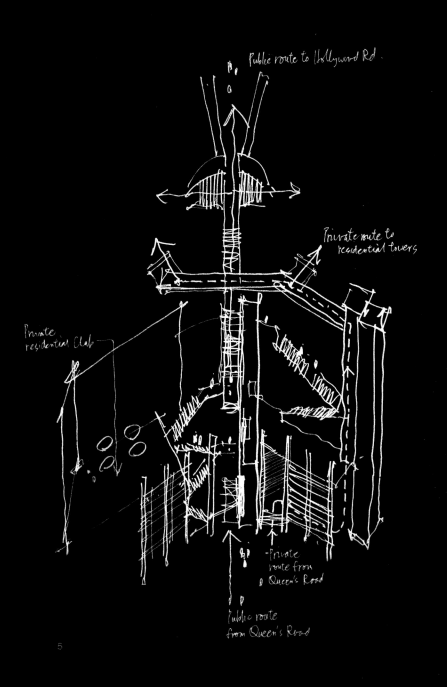

Public route to Hollywood Rd.

Private route to
residential towers

Private
residential Club

-Private
route from
Queen's Road

Public route
from Queen's Road

6

7

8

5   Concept sketch
6   View upwards from
    Queen's Road
7   Exterior view
8   View downwards
    towards Queen's
    Road, public stair to
    the left and private
    clubhouse terrace to
    the right

9

10

11

12

9　Landscaped
public passage
at Hollywood
Road level

10　View towards
Hollywood Road
from top landing
of public lifts with
private bridge
overhead

11　View along public
route towards
city

12　Top landing of
public lifts

13　View towards top
landing of public
lifts from private
bridge

13

14

14   Exterior detail
15–17
       Interiors of the private clubhouse in the podium

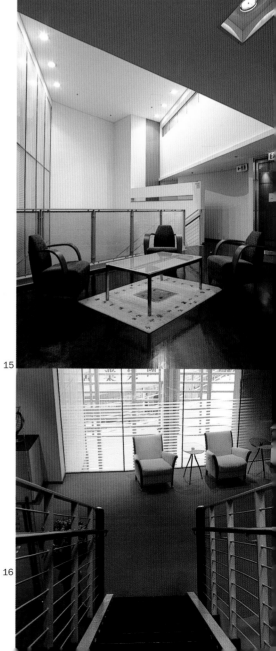

15

16

荷李活華庭

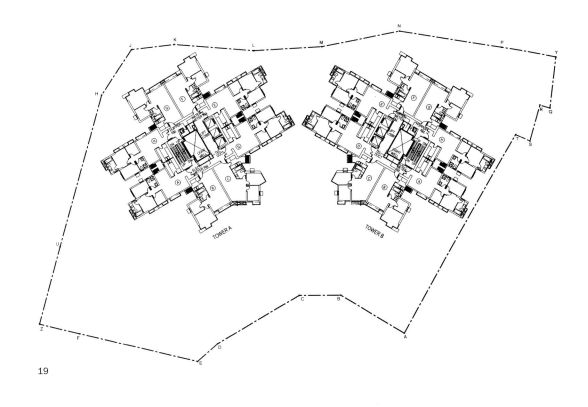

19

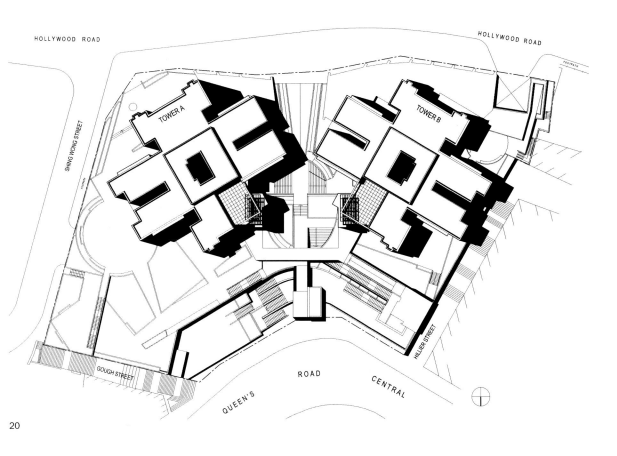

20

18 Podium nestled against the hill
between Hollywood Road at upper level
and Queen's Road at lower level
19 Podium level plan
20 Block plan

A corner tower that **relieves** the visual congestion by making
the **private** realm an **apparent extension** of the **public** one.

8 QUEEN'S ROAD CENTRAL

CENTRAL, HONG KONG
DESIGNED 1997, COMPLETED 2000
HKIA CERTIFICATE OF MERIT 2001

Straddled by Queen's Road Central and Ice House Street on a tight 612-square-metre corner site, the design of the building required a conscious response to one of the most frenetic intersections in Hong Kong's central business district.

The main entrance to the building is created as a transparent, two-storey glass volume of spatial simplicity, which embraces the bustling streetscape. The transparent part of the boundary allows the private realm to feel part of the public one, and the greenery of the neighbouring hillside still largely occupies one's vision while under the entrance canopy.

Inside, visual connectivity is established through the planning of spatial sequences. From the entrance glass volume, a pair of escalators lead to another two-storey-high lift lobby; another transparent volume top-lit by a crystal skylight, from which the natural light washes down a large beige wall surface, creating ever-changing shadows during the day, and allowing the spatial appearance to change with time, season and weather. Public and private spaces, always physically separated, are now virtually connected again.

Connectivity is apparent from the tower above to the pedestrians and vehicles on the street. Elevating the main lift lobby to the first floor has also enabled the best use of the gradient across the site with its relatively small footprint.

A bamboo garden is carved out onto a small flat roof next to the lifts in the main lobby. As the site is bounded by three streets, more natural light is drawn into the interior, and yet another, subtler connection is established with the city through this configuration. The theme of visual connectivity does not stop at the transparent enclosure of the lift lobby. While ascending, on every lift landing there are refreshing views of the former Government House, its garden and mature trees on the hill. This is achieved by placing the lift core structure at the perimeter of the site.

Solar control is adapted to different façades of the building, which experience different climatic conditions, either through their orientation or because sunshine is obscured by neighbouring buildings. The interlocking forms and silvery vertical fins of the tower deliver a distinctive urban texture to the corner of Ice House Street, especially in diffused sunlight.

Client: Sing Pao Investment Ltd.
Structural Engineer: Joseph Chow & Partners Ltd.
E/M Engineer: Meinhardt (M&E) Ltd.
Quantity Surveyor: Levett & Bailey
Main Contractor: Paul Y. - ITC Construction Ltd.
Construction Cost: HK$173 million

1

2

1,2
   Transparent entrance lobby at Ice House
   Street corner visually fusing the private
   realm with the public
3   First floor level
4   Typical office level
5   View of tower from Ice House Street

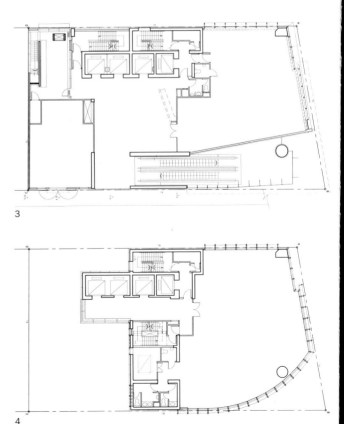

3

4

6   Typical lift lobby
with view and
natural lighting

7,8   First floor lobby
toplit by
skylight

9   First floor lobby,
escalators
down to
Queen's Road
on right

10   First floor lobby
looking towards
bamboo garden

As extension to an existing station that sits partially in the hillside; highly **permeable** to pedestrian access from all directions and fully **integrated** with the city.

LAI KING STATION

LAI KING, KOWLOON, HONG KONG
DESIGNED 1992, COMPLETED 1998

The station comprises a new station box running alongside an existing one, the new facility being essentially an extension of the original structure, integrated internally but independent structurally. Together they serve the two existing Tsuen Wan lines and the two new Tung Chung lines and accommodate the two new Airport Express lines as a pass-through.

The station is built partially into the hillside under Lai King Hill Road, and is part of the typically dense fabric of urban Hong Kong. The two critical planning issues are noise insulation/minimisation both during construction and operation, and access to/from neighbouring developments. A new pedestrian footbridge across Kwai Chung Road, which connects with a flight of stairs down from Lai King Hill Road provides the main access to the ticketing concourse for pedestrians from the Container Terminal to the west and Lai King Estate to the south. Internal flights of stairs and escalators lead people down to the concourse from Lai King Hill Road to the east, while pedestrian passages over the roof of the existing station link the residential neighbourhood to the northeast with the concourse. The station is thus highly permeable and integrated with the city.

While the old and new station boxes are in fact separate structures, there are two unifying elements in the architecture. One is the visually common base, clad in granite tiles and expressed as an artificial extension of the hillside behind, on which two tracks sit and into which four others penetrate. The other is the wide curvilinear roof over the new station, which sweeps past the new platform and partially overlaps the old station box. This roof provides noise protection by covering the open tracks and at the same time allows clerestory lighting on both sides to illuminate the new platform.

Client: Mass Transit Railway Corporation
Structural Engineer: Acer Consultants (Far East) Ltd.
E/M Engineer: Parsons Brinckerhoff (Asia) Ltd.
Quantity Surveyor: Davis Langdon & Seah (HK) Ltd.
Main Contractor: Maeda Corporation
Construction Cost: HK$700 million

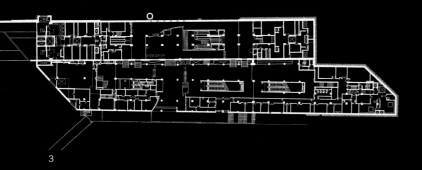

3

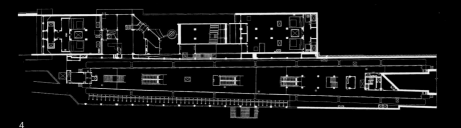

4

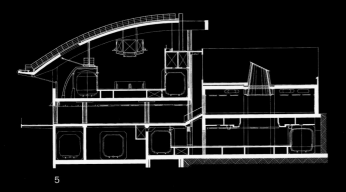

5

1 Model view, existing station box on the
left and new extension on the right
2 Sectional model
3 Lower level concourse plan
4 Upper level platform plan
5 Section

6 Exterior view, stair down from Lai King Hill Road in the foreground
7 Stair across from neighbouring housing estate
8 Overhead view, Lai King Hill Road in the background and bridges across Kwai Chung Road in the foreground

9

10

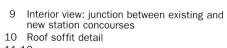

9 Interior view: junction between existing and
   new station concourses
10 Roof soffit detail
11,12
   Upper station platform with clerestory lighting

11

A new station that forms an **integral** part of a new town centre
in terms of movement pattern as well as visual identity.

TUNG CHUNG STATION
TUNG CHUNG, LANTAU, HONG KONG
DESIGNED 1992, COMPLETED 1998

Tung Chung Station is the terminus of the Tung Chung Line and was conceived as an integral part of the Tung Chung New Town. Being essentially a commuter station, its above-ground single-volume concourse discharges passengers right into the town's centre. One side of the station addresses the new town square, the town's community focus, while the other interfaces with a vehicular drop-off area. From the town square, two footbridges provide convenient linkage with the other parts of the town. One, a wide retail deck, springs across the North Lantau Expressway to link up with the residential development facing the waterfront. The other, a narrower elevated walkway, actually penetrates the station enclosure to link up the town square and the station with a public housing estate to the southeast.

The station's architecture is intended to set the tone for the spirit of the new community, emphasising simplicity and freshness. The main feature, the station roof, with a tapering and apparently uplifting soffit, is supported on two central rows of columns, which also taper to support the extensive cantilever. This frees up the peripheral enclosure as non-load-bearing, enabling a continuous glazing strip to run beneath the eaves all round and expanding into full-height glass walls at the concourse entrances at both ends. The visual lightness of the enclosure with its apparent detachment from the roof, its clear glazing and white metal cladding finish, is made to contrast with the robustness of the central columns, which are finished in fairfaced concrete.

Client: Mass Transit Railway Corporation
Structural Engineer: Over Arup & Partners
E/M Engineer: J Roger Preston Ltd.
Quantity Surveyor: Widnell Ltd.
Main Contractor: Aoki Corporation
Construction Cost: HK$245 million

1 Sectional
model;
footbridge in
the background
penetrating the
station
concourse
2 Part model
3 Exterior view
4 Entrance to
station from
town square
5 View of station
from town
square; public
housing
estates in the
background

6   Skylit entrance to station concourse
7   Exterior vent detail
8   Façade detail
9   Interior of concourse toplit by clerestory lighting

10 Entrance to station from town square
11 Footbridge link from public housing
 estate
12,13
 Exterior details

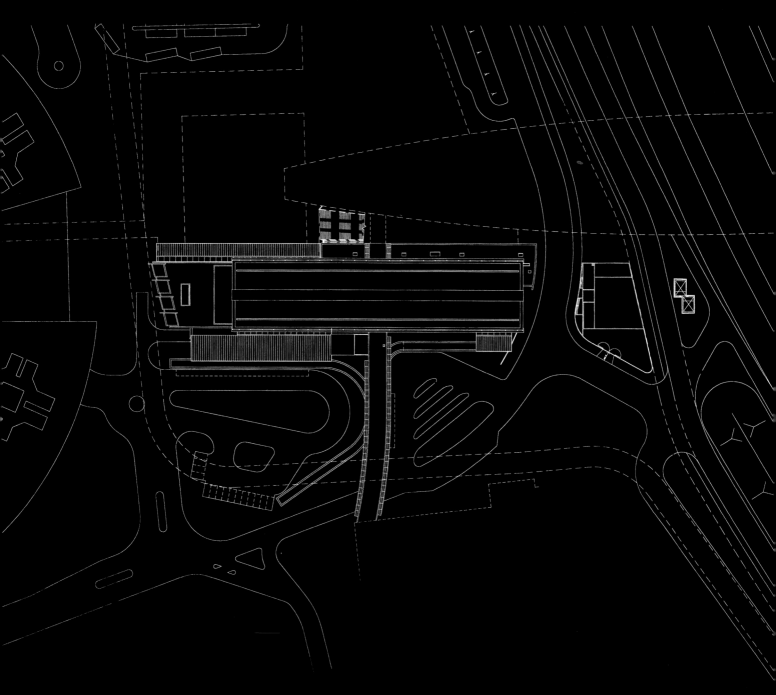

15

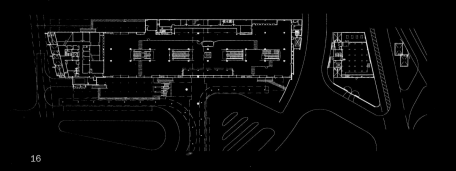

16

17

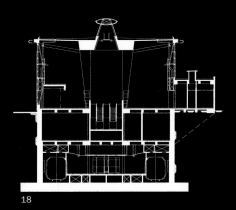

18

15   Block plan
16   Concourse level plan
17   Platform level plan
18   Section

The terminal station of the Airport Railway and associated development, a complex matrix of transport, public and commercial functions that is in itself a mini-city within the city.

HONG KONG STATION & DEVELOPMENT

CENTRAL, HONG KONG
PHASE 1 – DESIGNED 1995, COMPLETED 1998
HKIA CERTIFICATE OF MERIT 2000
PHASE 2 – DESIGNED 1998, COMPLETION EXPECTED 2004

Background

In January 1992, Rocco Design Ltd., in association with Anthony Ng Architects, was appointed by the Mass Transit Railway Corporation (MTRC) to develop the concept design for the entire series of stations along the Lantau Airport Railway. Back then, the fate of the so-called 'Rosegarden' venture, which included the Chek Lap Kok Airport and all the related infrastructural projects, still hung in the balance. The relationship between the British and Chinese Governments was then at its lowest point, and it would be another 34 months before a joint blessing was given to signify that the project would be undertaken. But politics aside, and even if all else went well, it was realised from the outset that architecturally it would be nothing short of a miracle in the extremely pragmatic and commercial cultural climate, which dominated Hong Kong, for the essence of the conceptual proposals to remain intact during the subsequent years of detailed design and development, when they would be subject to minute scrutiny and challenge by engineers and property developers. Together with the MTRC, the consultants developed not only a series of conceptual layouts and forms for the stations, but more importantly, established a set of design guidelines which ensured that all the stations, despite the inevitable design evolution and changes, would eventually share a distinct line identity and architectural ambience.

Central to these guidelines is the requirement that these stations should be transparent, fluid spaces that employ optimum natural illumination and clear spatial configuration to guide the movement of masses of commuters. In the case of Hong Kong Station, this was embodied in the In-Town Check-In (ITCI) Hall, the heart of the new building, where the dramatic four-storey-high space is lit by a full-height glazed wall to the north, and skylights/clerestory lighting from above. A series of large voids are immediately sited inside the glazed wall to allow natural light to penetrate the basement concourse, and these, at the same time, give a hint to commuters, immediately on entry, to the presence of the train platform.

Another crucial guideline in the concept design is that the stations should be firmly anchored in the city, and that an intimate interface, both visually and physically, should be established between the station and the station's commercial development, as well as with the surrounding urban fabric. In the context of Hong Kong Station, located right in the centre of the central business district on Hong Kong Island, this results in the overlay of a comprehensive pedestrian movement system onto the station footprint. This system operates at street level, subterranean level and, most importantly, at elevated deck level, linking up with the pedestrian walkway network already in place, which

Client: MTRC in association with
Central Waterfront Property Development Ltd.
Architects: Arup Associates in association with
Rocco Design Ltd.
Structural Engineer: Ove Arup & Partners (HK)
E/M Engineer: Meinhardt (M&E) Ltd.
Quantity Surveyor: Davis Langdon & Seah (HK) Ltd.
Main Contractor, Specialist Glazing and Steelwork:
Aoki Corporation

will eventually extend all the way to the new harbour front. The master layout plan, endorsed by the MTRC at this conceptual design stage, also stipulates the development of three office towers, two hotels and a retail podium. And it is the latter that will incorporate the deck-level pedestrian movement network that will wrap round both the ITCI Hall above the station departure concourse as well as the future Integrated Entrance Atrium above the station arrival concourse.

Looking back, this is a crucial phase of the design process, because not only were the MTRC's chief architect and the consultants involved, but most of the engineers and planners in the MTRC were also brought in to participate in the brainstorming sessions. Most of these people later went on to become crucial players in the implementation of the railway during detailed design and construction, some assuming project management roles, and others planning consultancy roles to help secure planning and development approvals from government. By being part of the early design process, they gave tacit acknowledgment and support to the concept, which became a very valuable starting point for all the hard work that was to follow.

1

1,2,5
    Spatial concept of stations
3   Map of airport railway line
4   Concept diagram
6–9
    Study model of station elements

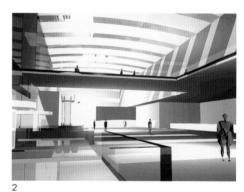

2

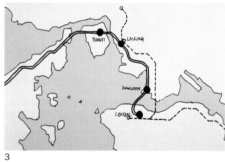

3

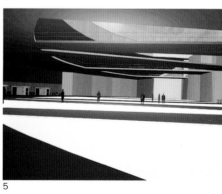

5

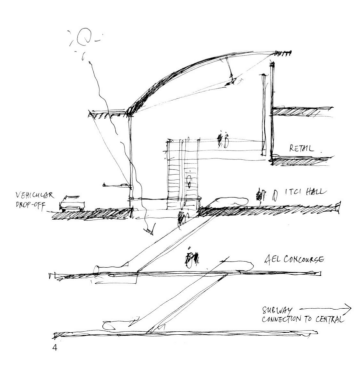

4

6 7

8 9

Hong Kong Station

Situated on the reclamation land in the central business district on Hong Kong Island, Hong Kong Station is the terminus of both the Airport Express and the Tung Chung Line and the Airport Railway's gateway to the heart of the city. As such, the station's links with new and existing transport and commercial facilities are crucial factors in the design.

The station is phase one of the substantial Central Reclamation property development, which will eventually comprise hotels, extensive retail facilities and office towers, including a landmark 88-storey building.

The station is also an important part of Central's comprehensive transport interchange. It connects with new and existing bus termini, the new ferry pier on the reclamation, drop-off points for private cars, buses and coaches, and perhaps most significant urbanistically, the existing elevated pedestrian walkways network in Central. An underground pedestrian link, the Central Subway, is also built between Hong Kong Station and the existing MTR Central Station to connect the two Airport Railway lines to the Island Line.

On a relatively constrained site, the station itself consists of five levels and functions, which are zoned accordingly.

The above-ground portion of the station consists mainly of the ITCI Hall, serving the Airport Express. This is the symbolic heart of the building and acts as the primary entrance to the station.

In accordance with common design concept guidelines for all the stations, the aesthetics of the ITCI Hall make optimum use of daylight and clarity of spatial configuration to assist circulation. The dramatic, four-storey-high space is topped by a curvilinear titanium roof, supported by a 12-metre column grid. Steel bowstring trusses support a full-height wall of glass along the seaward side of the building, facing the vehicular drop-off. The high degree of transparency of this central space, spanning the length of a city block, contrasts with the solid granite-clad bookends at the two ends of the station, which house vertical circulation spaces and elements for the retail floors at upper levels. From an urban design viewpoint, the two bookends relate to the podium of the adjacent Exchange Square while the transparent façade relates to the station forecourt and the future retail development across the drop-off area to the north.

A coherent structural order has been established for the steel elements, which form the roof trusses, glazing systems, canopies and footbridges throughout the station project.

The ground floor of the ITCI Hall houses the check-in desks for the Airport Express service. Glass elevators link the main concourse with mezzanine levels to the rear of the space, which contain retail facilities as well as 24-hour pedestrian connections with the rest of the city. Further commercial spaces are housed in the development nodes in the bookends, which also link the station to adjacent buildings. Glazed twin retail decks will link these bookends with the northern half of the station development in future.

Located immediately inside the main glass façade of the ITCI Hall are a series of large voids, which form a visual connection between the lower levels of the station and the ITCI Hall, bringing daylight into the arrival and departure platforms of the Airport Express, the heart of the station. Arriving passengers will be presented with a dramatic view up through the station to the ITCI Hall ceiling.

Vehicular access to the station is also provided at the south side of the building. After completion of the second phase, there will be separate platforms for arriving and departing passengers, each connected at the same level to taxi and private vehicle areas. In phase one however, only one platform is operational.

The level below the Airport Express platform is the Tung Chung Line concourse, which is connected via the Central Subway to the MTR Central Station. The Tung Chung Line platform is situated on the lowest level.

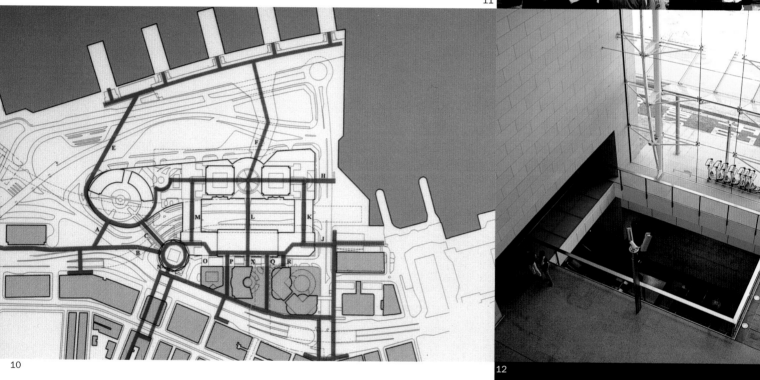

10

12

10 Original master layout plan showing existing and proposed footbridge network
11 View of station from Exchange Square Forum
12 ITCI hall interior
13 Overhead view of development

13

15

16

14 ITCI Hall, daylight penetrating the voids into the concourse below

15 Retail level above ITCI hall

16 Glazed entrance to station

17 Entrance bridges

18 View of ITCI hall from upper retail level

17

18

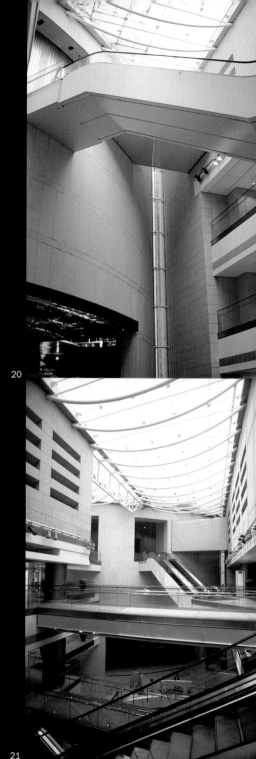

20

21

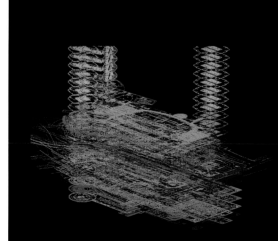

22

23

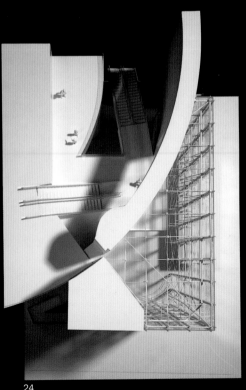

24

27

28

29

30

31

27–29
Details of
glass atrium
30,31
Connection
between
station on right
and Exchange
Square on left,
office entrance
atrium in
background
32 Pedestrian
connection
from existing
Connaught
Road
footbridge
33 Exterior view
of office and
podium

32

33

34

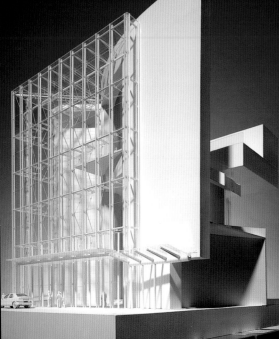

35

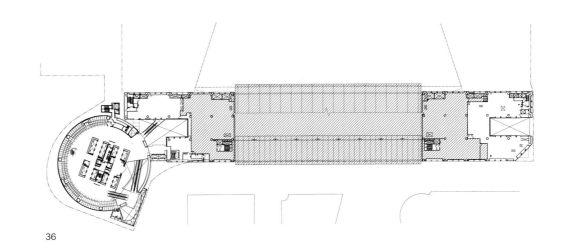

36

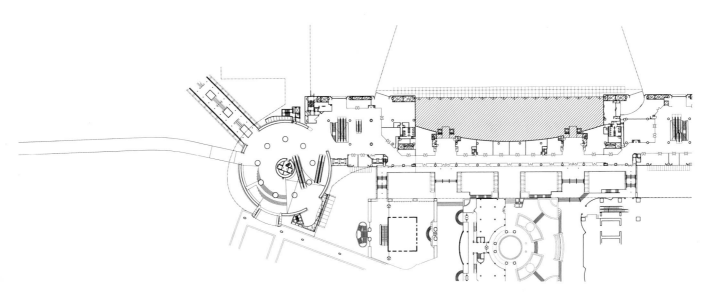

37

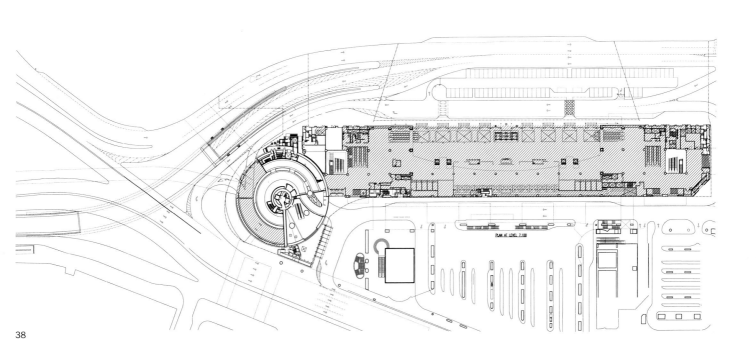

PLAN AT LEVEL 7.100

38

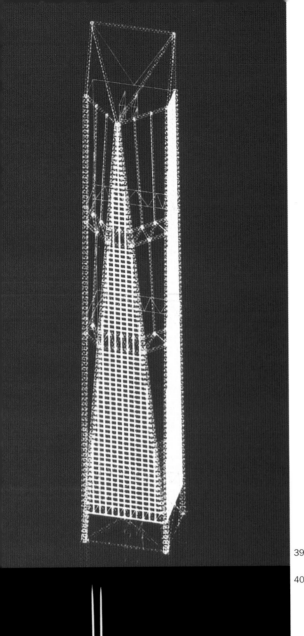

Hong Kong Station Development

In November 1995, when the MTR Corporation invited tenders for the development above the station, five developer consortia submitted proposals. Central Waterfront Property (P.M.) Ltd., which commissioned Rocco Design Limited as the architect, eventually won the bid.

As part of their tender proposal for the submission, Rocco advised the developer to consider in the master layout one major deviation from the Development Control Brief. The two office buildings on the northern site above the Arrival Hall would be combined into one single super-high-rise tower on the northeast corner. This is on the assumption that the Town Planning Board could be persuaded to waive its previous control on the height of buildings along the harbour front on a re-submission of the Master Layout Plan. Although the new northeast tower would protrude visually above the ridge-line of Victoria Peak when viewed from across the harbour and possibly be controversial, this revised layout would give a number of distinct planning and environmental advantages, and remove some of the crucial difficulties not satisfactorily resolved in the previous Master Layout Plan.

First, the restriction of the office tower footprint to the northeast corner, with its own entrance plaza, would minimise the interference to the station's access at ground level.

Second, the removal of one tower from the northern podium would mean significantly less structural intrusion onto the station facilities below ground and the retail spaces in the podium above. In particular, the major pedestrian movement network incorporated into the first level of the podium would become much more fluid and less restrictive.

Third, the podium roof, now substantially free of superstructure, could become a major public waterfront park.

Fourth, the visual permeability from the city out to the waterfront would actually be enhanced if there is one less 40-storey tower above the podium.

Finally, and not necessarily of least importance, the presence of a super-high-rise landmark tower denoting the location of Hong Kong Station, the terminal of the link to the city's international airport, is urbanistically appropriate.

Client: Central Waterfront Property Development Ltd.
Structural Engineer: Ove Arup & Partners
E/M Engineer: J. Roger Preston Ltd.
Quantity Surveyor: Levett & Bailey
Main Contractor: E. Man-Sanfield JV Construction Co Ltd.
Construction Cost: HK$13,608 million

39

40

41

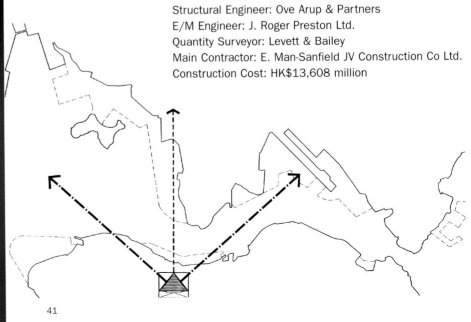

39–41
Design proposal for 400M tower, a design
that amalgamates structural form and view
orientation. Major structural elements in the
form of triangular moment-frame on each
façade diminish as the tower rises, opening
up structure-free façades to the northeast
and northwest, the direction towards which
the harbour stretches

42 Main pedestrian level in new master
plan layout plan
43 Typical mid-zone tower floor plan
44 400M tower in context

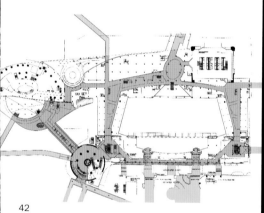

42

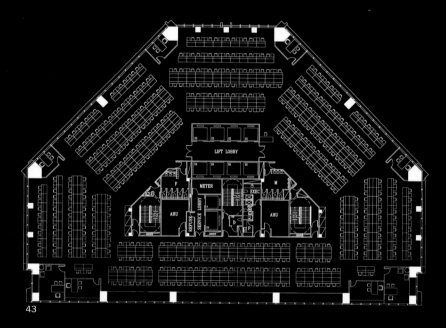

43

44

A stadium that **anchors** itself into the new town centre,
defying the traditional notion of a stand-alone structure.

PROPOSED FANLING INDOOR STADIUM

FANLING, NEW TERRITORIES, HONG KONG

DESIGNED 1994

Situated in one of the expanding new towns in the New Territories, the Fanling Indoor Stadium is the only major indoor venue for sports and cultural events in the district. The complex consists of a 5,000-seat main arena, a practice hall and related ancillary facilities. It is one of the first of a series of new public buildings to be built in an area adjacent to the Fanling Railway Station that is destined to become the future civic centre of the town. As such, the key factor in the design is as much what happens inside, dictated by fairly rigid dimensional and functional constraints of a sports venue, as what happens outside and around. The footprint of the architecture is a direct response to the axes of approach and fluidity of movement needed to serve large crowds. An elevated plaza deck receives them as they come across footbridges linking the railway station. From then on, a number of alternative routes bring them through and around the complex to the various other future public venues: the museum, the magistracy, the landscaped open space, and the existing market-place of the original township beyond. Together these routes form a network of connector bodies allowing the people to approach, to dissipate, to linger, to gather, to entertain or to engage in any other form of spontaneous activities that will, inevitably, be prompted or influenced by the mood of the architecture, and that contributes ultimately to the civic identity of the town.

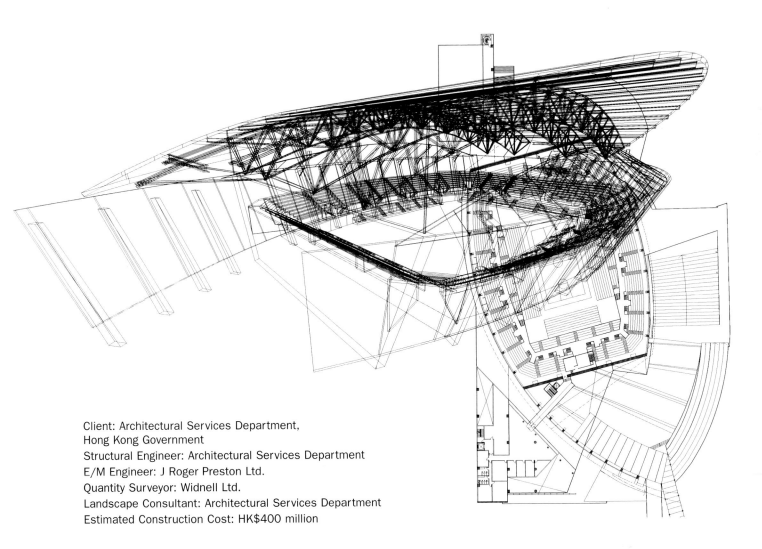

Client: Architectural Services Department,
Hong Kong Government
Structural Engineer: Architectural Services Department
E/M Engineer: J Roger Preston Ltd.
Quantity Surveyor: Widnell Ltd.
Landscape Consultant: Architectural Services Department
Estimated Construction Cost: HK$400 million

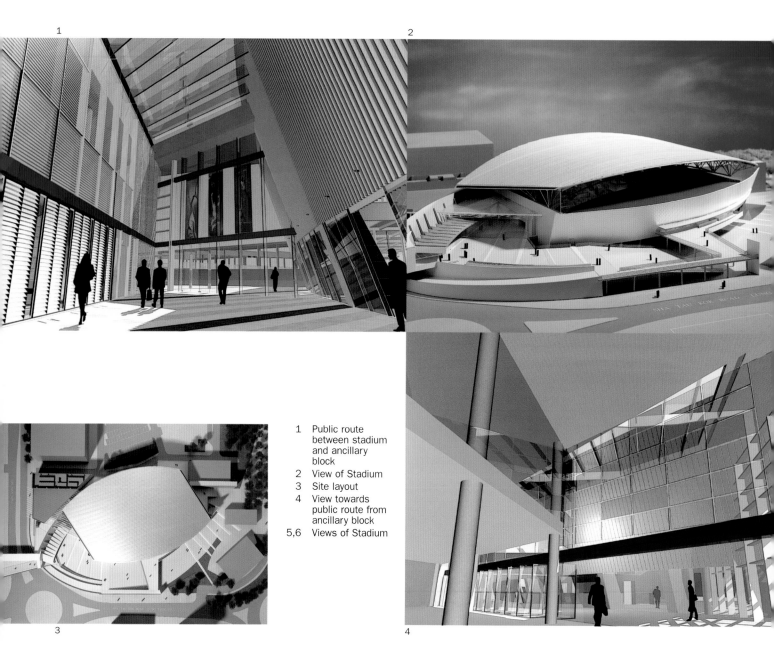

1 Public route
   between stadium
   and ancillary
   block
2 View of Stadium
3 Site layout
4 View towards
   public route from
   ancillary block
5,6 Views of Stadium

An **environmentally conscious** student hostel that **embraces** the campus.

STUDENT HOSTEL AT CHUNG CHI COLLEGE CHINESE UNIVERSITY OF HONG KONG

HONG KONG
DESIGNED 1999

The site for this new hostel for 300 students is at the eastern end of a residential square of Chung Chi College. Situated on a spur with a landscaped garden at its centre, the square has open views to Tolo Harbour and the hills of Ma On Shan to the east and a bird's eye view of Shatin New Town to the south. A footpath takes students down to the railway station through the site at its southern end.

The building is organized into two residential wings responding to the immediate environmental constraints by turning 90°, with the gable wall facing the motorway and the railway below. Together, they enclose a triangular courtyard. A single-loaded corridor provides both access and natural ventilation to the bedrooms. Ventilation through the building is further encouraged with the introduction of skygardens – landscaped terraces built at different levels to facilitate air movement across the building.

The building is arranged so as to allow for an unobstructed view of Ma On Shan from the landscaped garden. A cloister is laid out along the axis of the garden defining an entrance courtyard and sheltering the entrance lobby. The building is then elevated, with only the essential accommodations at ground level.

Within the confines of the cloister, a newly created amphitheatre is introduced along the footpath leading from the square to the station below. This forms part of the commuter route from the station to this part of the campus and its vicinity.

Taking advantage of the sloping site, the 'communal part' of the building is half submerged into the site, with game rooms, function rooms, a chapel and a multi-purpose hall facing the harbour. By virtue of their location, immediately adjacent to the commuter route, interaction with the general student body is encouraged.

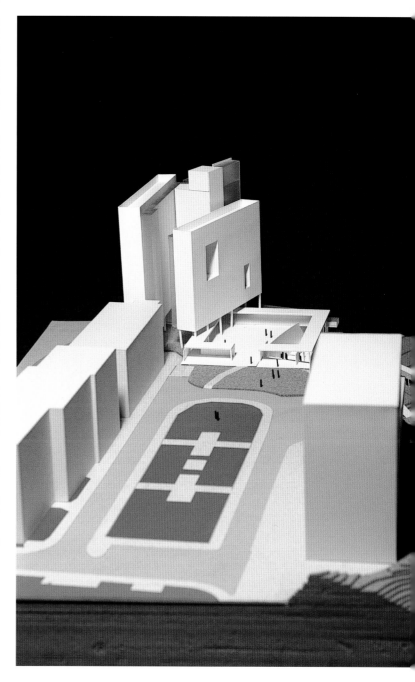

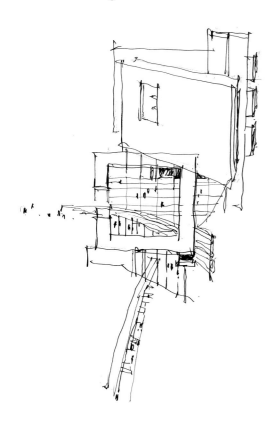

Client: Chinese University of Hong Kong
Structural Engineer: Wong & Cheng Consulting Engineers Ltd.
E/M Engineer: Campus Development Office, CUHK
Quantity Surveyor: Northcroft Hong Kong Ltd.
Estimated Construction Cost: HK$104.5 million

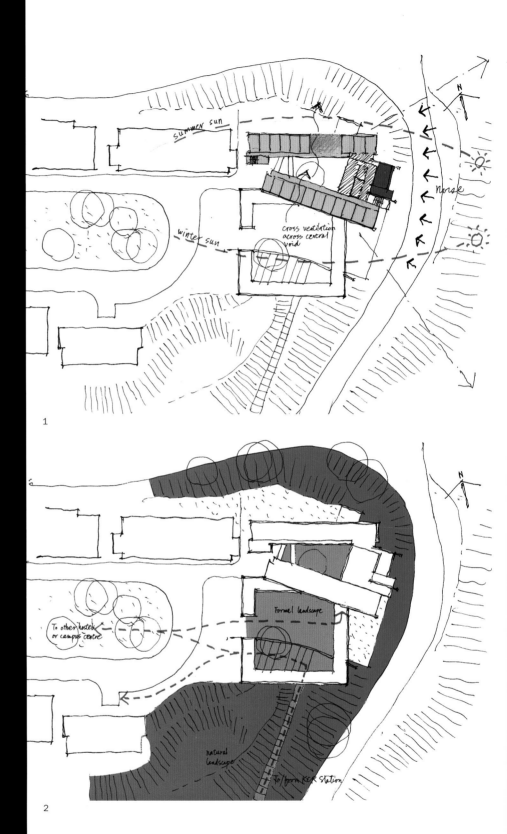

1

2

3

4

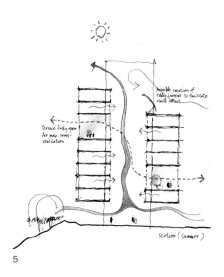

5

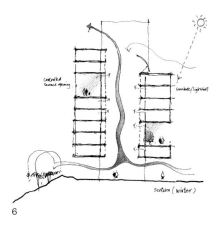

6

A return to **roots.**

THE BAMBOO PAVILION

FESTIVAL OF VISION
HONG KONG IN BERLIN
DESIGNED 1999, COMPLETED 2000
HKIA CERTIFICATE OF MERIT 2001

Traditionally, bamboo was a material held in special reverence in China, its characteristics being regarded as synonymous with the noble human qualities of resilience, honesty (being straight) and humility (being hollow in section).

As a building material, bamboo is still commonly used in Hong Kong in two main ways: scaffolding for construction and temporary structures. The latter are represented best by those open bamboo theatres that, during traditional festivals several times each year, are erected and dismantled, all within a matter of days.

It is both on account of its cultural association and its practical handling properties that, when a temporary pavilion was required for an outdoor performance venue and a symbolic focus for the Festival of Vision - Hong Kong in Berlin, bamboo was a natural choice of material.

But the use of bamboo and the adoption of the traditional technique of jointing – by binding and lashing with sheaths or wires – is as far as tradition goes. The configuration and structure of the pavilion is otherwise entirely contemporary, conceived with due consideration to the nature of the material, spatial aesthetics and context. Unlike those traditional structures, which are based on the principle of 'redundancy', that is employing many more members than are required using a rough Cartesian grid, the pavilion is meticulously set out and precisely engineered.

The Bamboo Pavilion is visually permeable, with the bamboo members being at once structure, enclosure and spatial delineator. Notwithstanding constraints in size and length of natural bamboo stems, it utilizes the fundamental structural concepts of triangulation and curvilinearity, to produce an inherently rigid, yet visually dynamic form that sits serenely above the body of reflective water outside the House of World Cultures.

Client: The Hong Kong Institute of Contemporary Culture
Structural Engineers: Ove Arup & Partners and
Bügler & Jaeck (Berlin)
Main Contractor: Gammon Construction Ltd
Construction Cost: HK$750,000

The two structures also form an interesting visual bond. While sharing certain common geometric generators, the house is monumental and permanent whereas the pavilion is light and ephemeral. While one is earthbound, the other is apparently floating. While one is largely opaque and solid, the other is permeable and transparent. While one is artificial, the other is natural. The House is definitely Western, the Pavilion originates more from the East. As a symbol of the Festival of Vision, the Pavilion aptly embodies its essence: a fusion of the traditional and the contemporary and a dialogue between West and East.

In all, roughly 400 pieces of bamboo were required for the project. They were sourced from the southern Chinese province of Guangxi, with strict requirements on size (approximately 120 millimetres diameter), so that the lateral setting-out could be achieved with reasonable precision, and on length (approximately 8 metres), so that the only longitudinal lap joint occurs at the top-spanning members (across a clear span of 18 metres). All the material specification and structural calculation have to follow the strict German codes and requirements and, before use, the bamboo members were straightened in China through heat and pressure, and further processed with insecticide and fire retardant.

Since the pavilion's form was alien to all the traditional bamboo workers (none of the members, for instance, was horizontal or vertical as in traditional bamboo structures), a prototype was first erected in Hong Kong for the workmen to practise on, and the same crew then went on to Berlin to execute the project.

Apart from its symbolic function, the pavilion was the venue for outdoor drama, music and fashion show events throughout the festival.

1

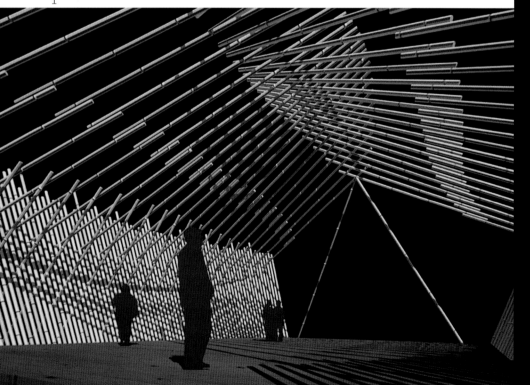

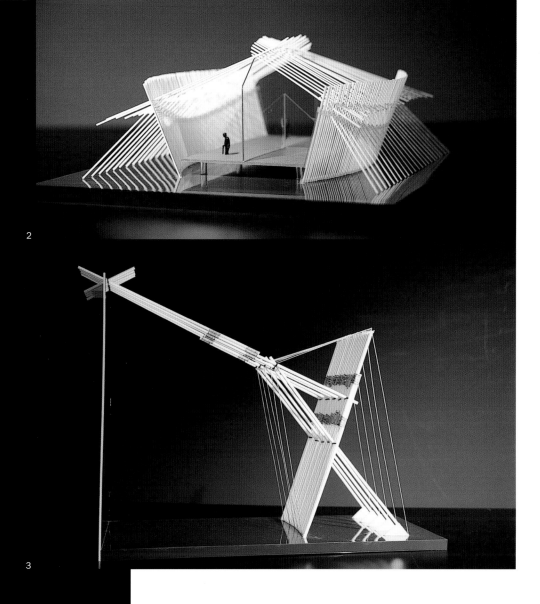

2

3

1   Computer image
2,4
    Study model, bamboo members precisely
    engineered to optimise their strength
3   Detailed construction model showing
    the concept of triangulation

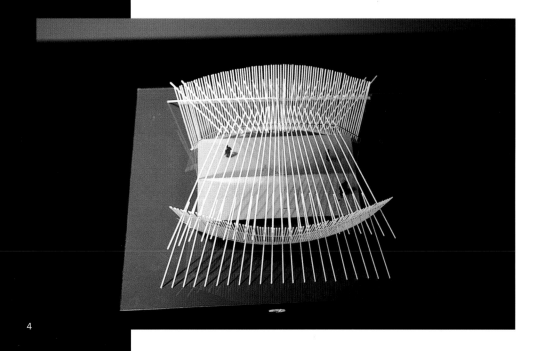

4

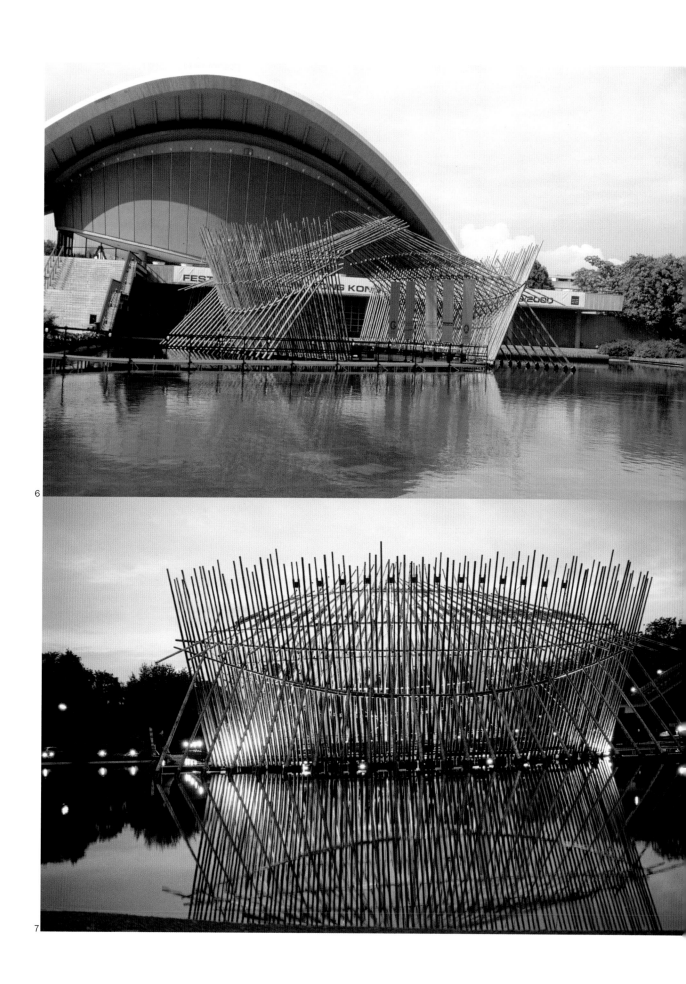

6

7

8

8,9
  Day and night views
10   Side elevation

9

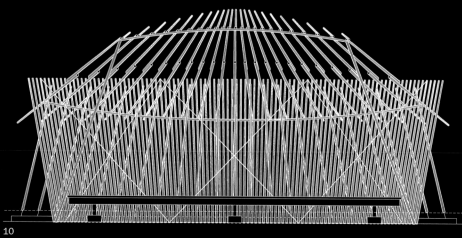

10

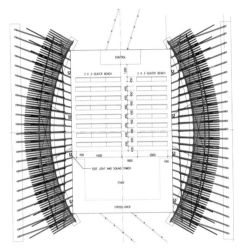

11

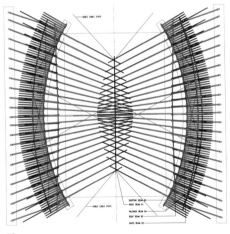

12

13

14

15

16

11 Layout plan
12 Roof plan
13 Front elevation
14–16
    Jointing details using mainly traditional
    methods of wire-lashing and binding, tensile
    cables to reinforce wind resistance

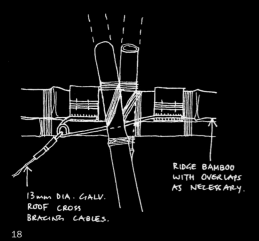

RIDGE BAMBOO
WITH OVERLAPS
AS NECESSARY.

13mm DIA. GALV.
ROOF CROSS
BRACING CABLES.

18

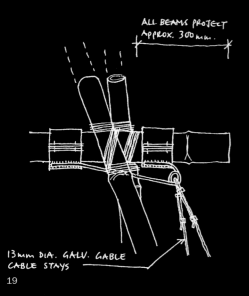

ALL BEAMS PROJECT
APPROX. 300mm.

13mm DIA. GALV. GABLE
CABLE STAYS

19

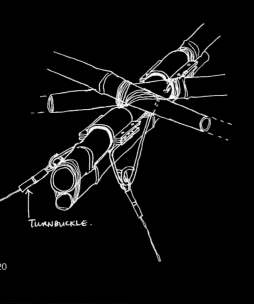

TURNBUCKLE.

20

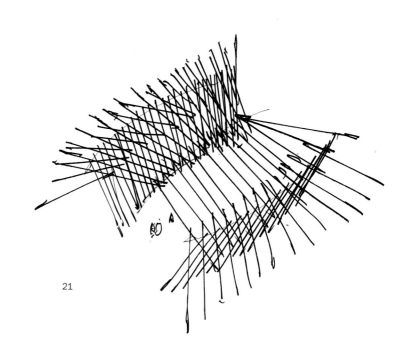

21

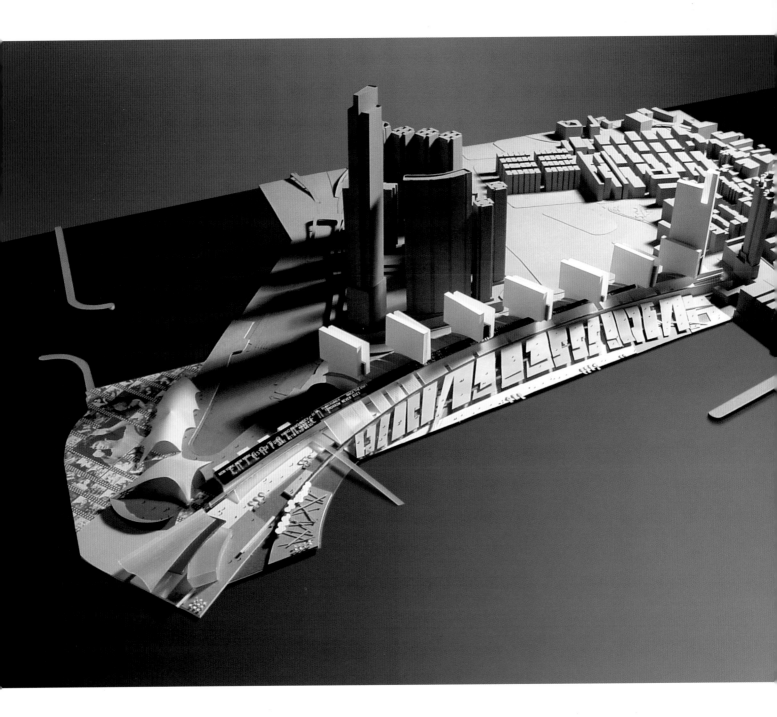

UPDATE

Rocco Design Limited has been awarded an Honourable Mention in April 2002 in an international competition to conceive a masterplan for an arts and cultural district on the reclaimed West Kowloon waterfront. The competition, launched in 1999, attracted a total of 161 entries.

The 10-member jury, which includes Prof. Chang Hsin-kang, Prof. Peter F.V. Droege, Prof. Patrick Lau, Prof. Peter G. Rowe, Prof. Wu Liangyong and Lord Rothschild as the chairman, said, "An Honourable Mention was given to this entry for its innovative design, and the unifying feature of a circulation spine connecting and providing access to all the many activities on the site. This design also took great advantage of a multi-level urban promenade along the waterfront. It also proposed an upbeat, media-oriented image and took explicit advantage of the site's location and public outlook back towards central Hong Kong. All in all, a very lively and compelling solution."

Projects in Progress 2002–

HARBOUR AS THE CENTRE

A new district for art and culture, **borne** of the city and **conceived** from its **relationship** with the harbour and the city's skyline.

WEST KOWLOON CULTURAL DISTRICT

WEST KOWLOON, HONG KONG

DESIGNED 2001
INTERNATIONAL COMPETITION, HONOURABLE MENTION

Hong Kong is an international city characterised by her immense density and dynamic transformation over time. The new Integrated Arts, Culture and Entertainment District captures the spirit of the city. It allows organic growth and embraces the richness of the urban fabric by creating neighbourhoods with mixed uses, streets and markets bustling with activity round the clock, and flexible indoor and outdoor spaces for shows, performances and festivities.

The city's harbour has always been Hong Kong's key public asset, a much-prided natural heritage of her people ever since the city was named after it as the "fragrant harbour". Because the site is strategically located along the waterfront, the new district embraces the harbour with a curved central spine, sustaining the symbolic reference of the harbour as the centre with streets and vistas orientated towards it.

The Peak, along with the mountain range that provides the backdrop of the city's dramatic skyline, is another special asset, which gives Hong Kong its much-prided identity.

The new district optimises opportunities for capturing the key vantage points for these natural and urban landmarks, enriching views and therefore memories of these places.

The district's urban form adopts the metaphor of a 'leaf', a symbol of birth, energy and organic growth. The main 'artery' of this leaf is the central spine, which serves as a major pedestrian circulation thoroughfare with a solar-powered electric trolley system connecting the entire district. The branching veins of this leaf are streets, their axes targeting specific landmarks across the harbour, emanating from the spine which sub-divides the different sections of the district. This system facilitates organic and incremental growth as well as providing efficient servicing.

The rooftops defined by the veins are conceived as landscaped parks above developments on the South Bank. They form a series of undulating 'green leaves' cascading towards the harbour and become a unique multi-level urban promenade along the waterfront, for the enjoyment of what surely is one of the most spectacular skylines in the world.

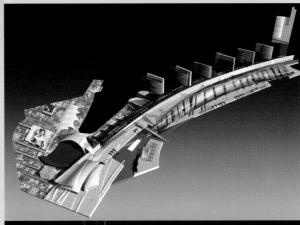

Client: The Government of Hong Kong SAR
Collaborators: Davis Lee, Perry Poon & Mathias Woo

A school that brings about maximum **interaction** among
students and with the outside **community** in
its pursuit of an inspired art education.

HK SCHOOL OF ART, MEDIA & DESIGN

KOWLOON TONG, HONG KONG

DESIGNED 2002

The School of Arts Media & Design is first and foremost a secondary school that provides teaching facilities for pre-university teenagers who aspire to an art education. At the same time, it is a community institution that shares its major facilities with the general public, in particular the 530-seat theatre and the 10,000-square-metre exhibition gallery and library. The architecture responds accordingly to this functional duality in its disposition and spatial organisation.

The site is located in an area of the city where up-market residential neighbourhoods meet low-cost public housing districts, and where institutional facilities flank the site on all sides including a district open space to the south. It is also located in between two major MTR stations one to the south and another to the north.

Central to the planning strategy is the introduction of a linear pedestrianised street, which runs north to south through the site to allow major access from both directions. This street is flanked by all the major functions anticipated to be shared by the community: lecture theatres, a library, exhibition gallery, cafeteria and a theatre, and will become the rallying element of the school. Spanning across it in the transverse direction, rather like bridges across a river, are the private teaching blocks comprising classrooms, crit rooms and special function rooms. This configuration enables students to go about their daily lessons without the need to mix with the public, yet at the same time result in an optimum visual and spatial interaction between them, heightening that sense of collective participation so essential a catalyst for artistic endeavours.

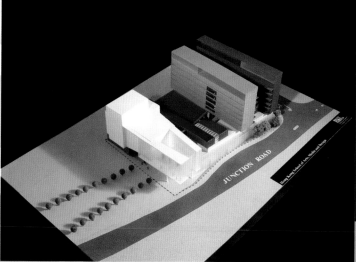

Client: The Hong Kong Institute of Contemporary Culture Ltd.
Structural Engineer: Greg Wong & Associates Ltd.
E/M Engineer: J Roger Preston Ltd.
Quantity Surveyor: Levett & Baliley Chartered Quantity Surveyors Ltd.

A teaching complex that serves the entire student body
not as much through its provision of facilities as
through the establishment of **connectivity** both physical and social.

COMPOSITE TEACHING BUILDING COMPLEX

THE CHINESE UNIVERSITY OF HK, SHATIN, N.T.

DESIGNED 2002

The project is a composite teaching building complex for the Chinese University of Hong Kong. Located right at the university's main entrance, the complex will be a multi-storey building with a gross floor area of approximately 10,000 square metres. It will comprise topical communal teaching facilities such as seminar/function rooms, classrooms and lecture theatres, a variety of teaching and research laboratories, as well as offices for staff and research personnel.

The design of the teaching complex aims to achieve the following key objectives:

- be a prominent landmark building with a strong identity at the main entrance to strengthen the role of the university in society

- be a modern teaching facility which encourages interdisciplinary interaction between staff and students to promote learning and forward thinking

- be a visual and physical extension of the mall setting of the central campus with opportunities for campus enhancement and improved pedestrian connection

- be the initial phase in renewing and redeveloping the area comprising the existing Leung Kau Kui Building, Fung King Hey Building and Li Dak Sum Building.

The teaching complex is more than just a building. It is also a continued effort by the university to enhance and consolidate the campus and represents a strategic phase in the CUHK Campus Redevelopment scheme.

Client: The Chinese University of Hong Kong
Structural Engineer: Meinhardt (C&S) Ltd.
E/M Engineer: Meinhardt (M&E) Ltd.
Quantity Surveyor: Levett & Bailey Chartered Quantity Surveyors Ltd.
Estimated Construction Cost: HK$157 Million

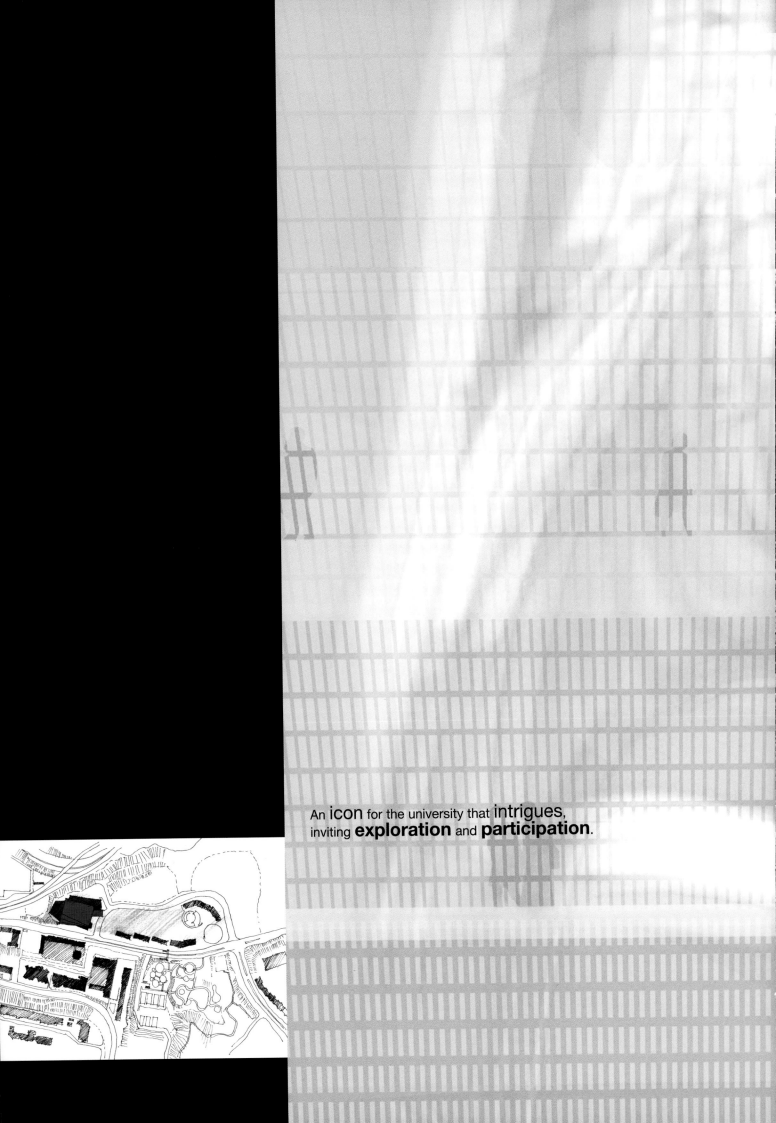

An icon for the university that intrigues,
inviting exploration and participation.

MULTI-MEDIA BUILDING

CITY UNIVERSITY, HONG KONG

INVITED COMPETITION 2002

As an icon for the City University, the Multi-Media Building is designed to emit a strong but simple message to communicate with the outside world.

Externally, the Multi-Media Building evokes the metaphor of a cocoon: an embryo being wrapped, protected and nurtured in an environment that nestles breakthroughs for radiant ideas. While the major 'black box' functions are clad in profiled dark granite as a visual extension of the surrounding hills, the protective 'skin' that seemingly wraps and nurtures these elements is in fact a glazed enclosure where the linear transom members delineate the curves and folds of the skin. Matt ceramic frit patterns, applied externally to the glass in carefully configured patterns of size and density, create varying conditions of opacity, translucency and transparency in the skin for visual as well as environmental reasons.

This particular cocoon is not quite the usual cocoon. Transcending its protective and incubative role, it lures and beckons visitors to explore its inner secrets and wonders within a large gaping hollow. This hollow is the WOMB: a space in which one feels wrapped round, nourished and inspired by its many moods, sights and sounds.

The WOMB is in fact a communal space where the visitor is surrounded by and therefore interacts with the building's movement systems – the grand ramp leading to the theatre with the student atrium above, and access corridors to the many public and student functions (eg. multi-media library, representation theatres and classrooms) on both sides.

The combination of opaque, translucent and transparent glass surfaces that envelope this space creates varying perceptions of spatial qualities at different times of the day as well as on varying occasions by the manipulation of relative internal and external lighting levels.

It is a three-dimensional stage-set where an infinite permutation of video projection configuration could be produced and experimented. The WOMB is an all-encompassing space for interaction. It is also a place to constantly intrigue, surprise and inspire.

Client: City University of Hong Kong
Structural/Geotechnical Engineer: Ove Arup & Partners Hong Kong Limited
Acoustics and Lighting: Arup Acoustics and Arup Lighting
IT and Telecommunications: Arup Communications
E/M Engineer: Meinhardt (M&E) Limited
Façade Engineering: Arup Facade
Estimated Construction Cost: HK$ 600 million

1981	HKIA Certificate of Merit for Franki Centre
1983	First Prize Award, International Competition for l'Opéra de la Bastille, Paris
1984	HKIA President's Prize for Mong Tung Wan Youth Hostel
1986	HKIA President's Prize for Pak Sha O Youth Hostel Extension
1986	Top 30 Citation, International Competition for Japan National Theatre, Tokyo
1989	Honourable Mention, International Competition for New Alexandria Library, Alexandria
1991	HKIA Certificate of Merit for Lok Fu Centre II
1994	ARCASIA Gold Medal for Lok Fu Centre II
1994	HKIA Silver Medal for Citibank Plaza
1995	HKIA Silver Medal for Peninsula Hotel Extension
1998	HKIA Silver Medal for HKU Graduate House
2000	HKIA Certificate of Merit for Hong Kong Station
2001	HKIA Certificate of Merit for Hollywood Terrace
2001	HKIA Certificate of Merit for 8 Queen's Road Central
2001	HKIA Certificate of Merit for Bamboo Pavilion, Berlin
2002	Honourable Mention, International Competition for West Kowloon Cultural District Concept Design

SELECTED CHRONOLOGY

1981   Franki Centre
Commercial Complex
Kowloon Tong, Hong Kong

1983   Mong Tung Wan Youth Hostel
Hong Kong

1985   Pak Sha O Youth Hostel
Sai Kung, Hong Kong

Parklane Shopping Boulevard
Nathan Road
Tsimshatsui, Hong Kong

1986   Residential Development
at Pollock Path, The Peak
Hong Kong

1988   Extension to Carmel English School
Homantin, Hong Kong

Interior Design for Hong Kong Convention & Exhibition Centre
Wanchai, Hong Kong

Residential/Commercial Complex
Ho Chung Marina
Hong Kong

Dragon Hotel
Hangzhou, China

Belleview Place
Residential Development
Belleview Drive
Repulse Bay, Hong Kong

Tai Mo Shan Youth Hostel Extension
Tsuen Wan, Hong Kong

International Exhibition Centre   1989
Tientsin, China

Church & Kindergarten Building
Fanling, Hong Kong

Hong Kong Tramways
East & West Depots
Hong Kong

Motorola Silicon Harbour Centre   1990
Tai Po, Hong Kong

Extension of
Legislative Council Chambers
Central, Hong Kong

1991   Lok Fu Shopping Centre II
        Lok Fu, Kowloon, Hong Kong

1992   Residential Development
        4 Peel Rise
        The Peak, Hong Kong

        School for the Mentally Handicapped
        Fairview Park
        Yuen Long, Hong Kong

        Citibank Plaza
        I.L. 8888 Garden Road
        Hong Kong

1993   Tregunter Tower III
        Residential Development
        Mid-levels, Hong Kong

        Beijing Hilton Hotel
        Beijing, China

1994   Clovelly Court
        Residential Development,
        12 May Road
        Mid-levels, Hong Kong

        Peninsula Hotel Extension
        Tsimshatsui, Hong Kong

Hanley Villa
Residential Development
Yau Kam Tau, Hong Kong

Wu York Yu Care and Attention Home
Shuen Wan, Hong Kong

Commercial & Office Building   1995
12 Ngan Mok Street
North Point, Hong Kong

Regional Services Department   1996
Vehicle Depot
Tai Po, Hong Kong

Residential Development
48 Mount Kellett Road
Hong Kong

Precious Blood Girls' School
Chai Wan, Hong Kong

Nanyin Tower Office Building   1997
Beijing, China

Oterprise Square
Commercial & Office Building
Nathan Road, Kowloon, Hong Kong

Shek Kip Mei Park Indoor Games Hall
Kowloon, Hong Kong

1998   Lantau & Airport Railway
        Hong Kong Station & Development (Phase 1)
        Central, Hong Kong

        Lantau & Airport Railway
        Lai King Station
        Lai King, Kowloon, Hong Kong

        Lantau & Airport Railway
        Tung Chung Station
        Tung Chung, Lantau, Hong Kong

        Graduate House
        The University of Hong Kong
        Pokfulam, Hong Kong

        Hang Seng Bank Branch Building
        Causeway Bay, Hong Kong

        Residential Development
        26 Mount Kellett Road
        The Peak, Hong Kong

1999   Man Yee Building
        Central, Hong Kong

        Hollywood Terrace
        Urban Renewal Development
        Hollywood Road, Hong Kong

Serenity Place
Sandwiched Class Housing
Tseung Kwan O, Hong Kong

Delta House
Industrial & Office Building
Shatin, Hong Kong

The Bamboo Pavilion   2000
Berlin

Consumer Council Regional Office
and Information Centre
Tsimshatsui, Hong Kong

Office Building
8 Queen's Road Central
Central, Hong Kong

Office Building
325 Lockhart Road
Wanchai, Hong Kong

Hong Kong Station & Development   2001 and
Central, Hong Kong   onwards
(current)

West Rail, 3 Railway Stations
Yuen Long Section
New Territories, Hong Kong

COMPANY PROFILE

Rocco Design Limited is a Hong Kong-based multi-disciplinary architectural firm, which over its past two productive decades, has established a solid pool of technical, practical and administrative expertise, but at the same time retained a youthful spirit and prowess for design creativity.

The firm has been in practice for over 20 years. Rocco S.K. Yim, founder of its predecessor firm, Rocco Design Associates, has practised since March 1979. Patrick P.W. Lee joined Rocco Design Partners in June 1980. In June 1982, Bernard M.B. Hui joined the partnership. Hector Cheung, C.M. Chan, Arthur Tsang and Clement Wong are directors of the current practice.

The firm currently employs about 180 staff. The main architectural section is supported by an interior design section, a building services engineering section, a model/graphics section and the latest CADD facilities.

The main objective of the firm is to provide comprehensive professional services, with the directors actively participating in all aspects of the projects, from conceptual design through to implementation and completion. Emphasis is placed on the innovation and practicality of design, balanced by an alertness to the construction budget and programme control, a sensitivity to clients' needs and aspirations and a consciousness of the quality of the total environment.

BIOGRAPHIES

Bernard M.B. Hui

B.A.A.S., B.Arch.(Dist.), FHKIA, RIBA
Registered Architect, AP(Architect)

Bachelor of Arts in Architectural Studies, HKU	1970
Assistant Architect, Leigh & Orange Architects & Engineers	1971
Joined Wong & Ouyang & Associates	1972–74
Bachelor of Architecture (Distinction), HKU	1976
Member of HKIA	1977
Rejoined Wong & Ouyang & Associates as Limited Partner	1977–82
Authorised Person – Architect	1978
Director of Rocco Design Limited	1982
Council Member of HKIA	1983–86, 1995–98, 2000
Hon. Secretary of HKIA	1987–88
Member of Construction Industry Training Authority	1991–97
Member of Pneumoconiosis Compensation Fund Board	1992–97
Vice President of HKIA	1993–94, 2001–02
Member of Advisory Committee on Building and Real Estate The Hong Kong Polytechnic University	1994–99
Chairman of Board of Internal Affairs, HKIA	1995–98
Honorary Lecturer	1994–98
Part-time Lecturer	1995–99
Honorary Associate Professor	2001–02
Department of Architecture, HKU	

Patrick P.W. Lee

B.Arch., HKIA, RIBA, FRAIA, ARBUK
Registered Architect, AP(Architect)
Chartered Architect

Bachelor of Architecture, HKU	1967
Associate of Royal Institute of British Architects	1969
Joined Architectural Office, PWD as Architect	1970
Senior Architect, Architectural Office, PWD	1975–80
Acting Chief Architect, Architectural Office, PWD	1979
Joined Rocco Design Partners	1980
Member of HKIA	1981
Authorised Person – Architect	1981
Director of Rocco Design Limited	1982

Rocco S.K. Yim

B.A.A.S.(Hons.), B.Arch.(Dist.), FHKIA, RIBA
Registered Architect, AP(Architect)

Bachelor of Architecture (Distinction), HKU	1976
Joined Spence Robinson Architects & Engineers	1976–79
Member of HKIA	1978
Authorised Person – Architect	1979
Founded Rocco Design Associates	1979
Director of Rocco Design Limited	1982
Council Member of HKIA	1987
Hon. Treasurer of HKIA	1989–90
Vice President of HKIA	1991–92
External Examiner Department of Architecture, HKU	1991–93
Member of Architects Registration Board	1992
HKIA Representative to ACABAS	1993
Member of AP/RSE Registration Committee	1994–97
Member of Energy Efficiency Advisory Committee (New Buildings Working Group)	1994
Vice Chairman Architects Registration Board	1995–97
Chairman Architects Registration Board	1997–98
Chairman Authorised Persons Registration Committee	1997
Honorary Professor in Architecture, HKU	1998
Member of Art Development Council	2000

DIRECTORS AND ASSOCIATES

C.M. Chan

Y.M. Chang

Joseph H.Y. Cheng

Hector Y.K. Cheung

Wicky F.K. Choi

Henry T.H. Ho

Bernard M.B. Hui

Dicky K.F. Lai

Jimmy W.H. Lee

Patrick P.W. Lee

William W.L. Tam

Arthur F.C. Tsang

Herrick H.K. Tsang

Mabel L.P. Tse

Chris C.L. Wan

Clement K.L. Wong

Rocco S.K. Yim

ARCHITECTS AND DESIGNERS

Patrick J. Adey

Paul T. Casey

Christina Y.Y. Chan

Dennis H.M. Chan

Pusey T.Y. Chan

Rava H.W. Chan

Frankie L.K. Cheng

Nacy M.S. Cheng

Franklin P.S. Cheung

Nelson C.F. Choi

Rebecca P.Y. Chung

Eric K.N. Ho

Antony Y.L. Kay

Charles S.C. Kung

Vincent Y.M. Kwan

K.C. Kwok

Vincent K.T. Kwong

Roy K.W. Law

Connie H.N. Lee

H.M. Lee

William C.F. Lee

Grace K.Y. Lin

Boris C.H. Lo

K.L. Lo

T.F. Lo

Jacky H.F. Lok

Anna K.F. Lui

William C.W. Ng

Ambrose K.M. Tang

Derrick K.L. Tsang

Ariel H.C. Tse

Andrew J. Reid

M.L. Yung

SELECTED BIBLIOGRAPHY

Opéra de la Bastille

Architectural Review (UK, December 1983).

Architects' Journal (UK, September 1983).

Le Monde de la Musique (France, October 1983).

Techniques & Architecture (France, November 1983).

Vision, Architecture Design (Hong Kong, No. 17, 1984).

Vision, Architecture Design (Hong Kong, 1986).

Wettbewerbe Aktuell (April 1984).

World Architecture Review (China, March 1994).

"L'Opéra de la Bastille." Electa Moniteur (France, 1989).

Pak Sha O Youth Hostel

Vision, Architecture Design (Hong Kong, 1986).

World Architecture Review (China, March 1994).

Tai Mo Shan Youth Hostel

World Architecture Review (China, March 1994).

Contemporary Architecture in Asia (ARCASIA) (1994).

Parklane Shopping Boulevard

Building Journal (Hong Kong, February 1986).

Vision, Architecture Design (Hong Kong, 1986).

World Architecture Review (China, March 1994).

Belleview Place

Art in America (July 1993).

World Architecture Review (China, March 1994).

Contemporary Architecture in Asia (ARCASIA) (1994).

Hollywood Terrace

Building Journal (Hong Kong, April 2002).

Building Review (Hong Kong, October 1999).

Hinge (Hong Kong, Vol. 38).

Hinge (Hong Kong, Vol. 67).

Citibank Plaza

Architecture and Urbanism (Hong Kong, March 1992).

Building Journal (Hong Kong, July 1992).

Dialogue (Taiwan, July 1997).

HKIA Journal (Hong Kong, 2nd Quarter, 1995).

Pace (Hong Kong, April 1993).

Space (Hong Kong, May 2001).

World Architecture Review (China, March 1994).

"Architectural Promenade." Arco Editorial s.a. (Spain, 1998).

Asian Style – 築摩書房株式會社, Japan

Contemporary Architecture in Asia (ARCASIA) (1994).

Hong Kong—City of Vision, Hinge Marketing Ltd. (Hong Kong, 1995).

Serving and Sloping Hong Kong, The University of Hong Kong (1999).

Skylines of Hong Kong, FormAsia Books Limited (Hong Kong).

Tall Buildings of Asia & Australia, The Images Publishing Group Pty Limited (Australia, 2001).

The Architecture of Skyscrapers, Hearst Books International (USA, 1997).

The World of Contemporary Architecture, Konemann Verlagsgesellschaft mbH (Germany, 2000).

Lok Fu Centre II

Building Journal (Hong Kong, March 1992).

Pace (Hong Kong, April 1992).

World Architecture Review (China, March 1994).

Fanling Stadium

Building Journal (Hong Kong, February 1998).

Dialogue (Taiwan, July 1997).

HKIA Journal (Hong Kong, 4th Quarter, 2001).

Hinge (Hong Kong, Vol. 36).

Hong Kong Station & Development

Architecture Record (USA, November 1998).

Architectural Review (UK, May 1999).

Building Journal (Hong Kong, October 1996).

Building Journal (Hong Kong, June 1997).

Building Journal (Hong Kong, August 1998).

Construction Review (Hong Kong, March 1999).

HKIA Journal (Hong Kong, 2nd Quarter, 2001).

Hinge (Hong Kong, Vol. 56).

Pace (Hong Kong, August 1998).

Space (Hong Kong, January 2000).

Space (Hong Kong, May 2001).

Hong Kong—City of Vision, Hinge Marketing Limited (Hong Kong, 1995).

Skylines of Hong Kong, FormAsia Books Limited (Hong Kong).

Tall Buildings of Asia & Australia, The Images Publishing Group Pty Limited (Australia, 2001).

The Bamboo Pavilion

Architectural Review (UK, January 2001).

Area (Italy, Vol. 58).

Architecture and Urbanism (Hong Kong, January 2001).

Building Journal (Hong Kong, April 2002).

Space (Hong Kong, August 2000).

ZOO (UK, Vol. 7, November 2000).

Oterprise Square

Architectural Record Pacific Rim (USA, No.7, 1994).

Architecture and Urbanism (Hong Kong, August 1998).

Domus (Italy, October 1998).

Hinge (Hong Kong, Vol. 54).

Building Enclosure in Hong Kong, Hong Kong University Press (Hong Kong, 1998).

Tall Buildings of Asia & Australia, The Images Publishing Group Pty Limited (Australia, 2001).

Graduate House

AIA Hong Kong (June 1999).

Architecture Asia (ARCASIA) (September 1999).

CAA—Commonwealth Association of Architects (June 1999).

Construction (May 1999).

Hinge (Hong Kong, Vol. 59).

Trends of Hong Kong Design (Singapore, Vol. 15, No. 2).

AWA—Architecture Optimal Award Winning Architecture International Yearbook 1999–2000, Sedlacek Vertag (Germany, 1999).

Serving and Sloping Hong Kong, The University of Hong Kong (1999).

West Kowloon Reclamation Competition

Architectural Review Australia (Autumn 2002).

Architecture and Urbanism, (Hong Kong, April 2002).

Building Journal (Hong Kong, March 2002).

General Articles

Arch (Hong Kong, No. 12).

Glass and Architecture (Japan, June 1992).

Innovative Architecture in Asia, Architectural Institute of Japan (1996).

Pace (Hong Kong, October 1997).

Weekly Asahigraph (Japan, 8 December, 1994).

SD—Space Design (Japan, No. 9702).

a-n (Japan No. 42, Winter, 1992).

581 Architects in the World, Atsushi Sato (Japan, 1995).

CREDITS

Mong Tung Wan Youth Hostel
Raymond Leung, K.M. Tam
Rocco Yim

Pak Sha O Youth Hostel
Raymond Leung, K.M. Tam
Rocco Yim

Parklane Shopping Boulevard
Bernard Hui, Finola Ng
Y.S. Tang, Rocco Yim

Pollock Path Residential Development
David Au, Bernard Hui
William Ko, Rocco Yim

Extension to Carmel English School
Bernard Hui, Patrick Lee
Rocco Yim, T.C. Yuen

Interior Design for Hong Kong Convention and Exhibition Centre
Trajn Bonghan, Trilby Choi
Herrick Tsang, Rocco Yim

Ho Chung Marina Residential/Commercial Complex
Bernard Hui, Rocco Yim, T.C. Yuen

Dragon Hotel, Hangzhou
Bernard Hui, H.M. Leung
Herrick Tsang, Rocco Yim

Belleview Place
David Au, Eddie Chung
Bernard Hui, Patrick Lee, Rocco Yim

Tai Mo Shan Youth Hostel
Raymond Leung, K.M. Tam
Rocco Yim

International Exhibition Centre, Tientsin
Eddie Chung, Patrick Lee
Tammy Wu, Rocco Yim

Church and Kindergarten Building at Fanling
Dicky Lai, Finola Ng,
Rocco Yim

Motorola Silicon Harbor Center
Wicky Choi, Bernard Hui
Rocco Yim

Extension of Legislative Council Chambers
Trilby Choi, Herrick Tsang
Rocco Yim

Lok Fu Centre II
Calvin Ho, Patrick Lee
Rocco Yim, Timothy Yuen

School for the Mentally Handicapped at Fairview Park
Hector Cheung, Bernard Hui
Peter Lee, Rocco Yim

Citibank Plaza
C.M. Chan, Hector Cheung, Trilby Choi
Bernard Hui, Patrick Lee, David Wong
Rocco Yim

Tregunter Tower III
Alex Chan, Hector Cheung, Bernard Hui
Patrick Lee, Alan Leung, Rocco Yim, T.C. Yuen

Hilton Hotel, Beijing
Bernard Hui, Patrick Lee, H.M. Leung
Rocco Yim, T.C. Yuen

Clovelly Court
Alex Chan, Bernard Hui
T.C. Yuen

Peninsula Hotel Extension

Hector Cheung, Eddie Chung, Calvin Fung

David Gibb, Bernard Hui, Manny Ing, Victor Lam

Lawrence Malek, John Tieh, Clement Wong

Rocco Yim

Hanley Villa

David Chan, Bernard Hui, Patrick Lee

H.M. Leung, Rocco Yim

Wu York Yu Care and Attention Home

Peter Lee, Finola Ng, Rocco Yim

Office Building at 12 Ngan Mok Street

Wicky Choi, Dicky Lai

Peter Lee, Rocco Yim

Regional Services Department Vehicle Depot

Hector Cheung, Johnny Li

Rocco Yim

48 Mount Kellett Road

Dick Fong, Bernard Hui

Patrick Lee, T.C. Yuen

Precious Blood Girls' School

Alex Chan, Hector Cheung

Bernard Hui, Johnny Li, Rocco Yim

Nanyin Tower, Beijing

Trilby Choi, M.C. Chung, Dicky Lai

Victor Lam, Patrick Lee, William Tam

Rocco Yim

Shek Kip Mei Park Indoor Games Hall

David Chan, William Lee

Rocco Yim

Lai King Station

C.M. Chan, David Chan

William Lee, Rocco Yim

Tung Chung Station

C.M. Chan, Chris Wan

Rocco Yim

Oterprise Square

C.M. Chan, Bernard Hui, Lawrence Malek

Chris Wan, Rocco Yim

Graduate House

David Chan, Hector Cheung, Bernard Hui

Charles Kung, Johnny Li, Grace Lin

Tony Pannell, Herrick Tsang, Rocco Yim

Hang Seng Bank Branch Building

C.M. Chan, Bernard Hui

Charles Kung, Michael Mak, Rocco Yim

26 Mount Kellett Road

Wicky Choi, Patrick Lee, Rocco Yim

Man Yee Building

C.M. Chan, Bernard Hui

Manny Ing, Grace Lin, Alejandro Tsang

Herrick Tsang, Rocco Yim

Hollywood Terrace

Joseph Cheng, Hector Cheung, David Gibb

Joey Ho, Bernard Hui, Patrick Lee

Johnny Li, Irene Wan, Rocco Yim

Serenity Place

Hector Cheung, Calvin Fung

Bernard Hui, Rocco Yim

Delta House

Hector Cheung, Wicky Choi

Bernard Hui, William Tam

Rocco Yim

The Bamboo Pavilion

Martin Fung, W.H. Lee

William Tam, Rocco Yim

8 Queen's Road Central

Hector Cheung, Wicky Choi,

Bernard Hui, Susanna Kwok, W.H. Lee,

Ambrose Tang, Herrick Tsang, Rocco Yim

325 Lockhart Road

C.M. Chan, Bernard Hui

Johnny Li, Chris Wan, Rocco Yim

Hong Kong Station & Development

C.M. Chan, Lawrence Chan, Pusey Chan

Joseph Cheng, Hector Cheung, Henry Ho

Bernard Hui, Anthony Kay, Charles Kung

Vincent Kwong, Patrick Lee, W.H. Lee

Dora Leung, Louis Leung, Grace Lin

Kent Lui, William Tam, Derrick Tsang

Herrick Tsang, Irene Wan, Clement Wong

Rocco Yim, M.L. Yung

West Rail Three Railway Stations

Paul Casey, C.M. Chan, Kin Choy

Bernard Hui, William Lee, Kent Lui

Andrew Reid, Rocco Yim

Fanling Indoor Stadium

Y.M. Chang, Manny Ing, Susanna Kwok

William Tam, Arthur Tsang, Rocco Yim

Student Hostel for Chinese University

William Tam, Rocco Yim

Every effort has been made to trace the original source of copyright material
contained in this book. The publishers would be pleased to hear from copyright
holders to rectify any error or omissions.

The information and illustrations in this publication have been prepared and supplied
by Rocco Design Limited. While all reasonable efforts have been made to ensure
accuracy, the publishers do not, under any circumstances, accept responsibility for
errors, omissions and representations express or implied.